In 1944, the thirteen-year old
Marlene Wiemer embarked on a
West, to escape the advancing Red Army. Her cousin
Jutta was left behind the Iron Curtain, which severed
the family bonds that had made the two so close.

This book contains dramatic depictions of Marlene's
chaotic flight, recreated from her letters to Jutta during
the last year of the war, and contrasted with joyful
memories of the innocence that preceded them.

Nearly fifty years later, the advent of perestroika
meant that Marlene and Jutta were finally able to
revisit their childhood home, after a lifetime of
growing up under diametrically opposed societies, and
the book closes with a final chapter revealing what
they find.

Despite depicting the same time and circumstances
as "Reflections in an Oval Mirror", an account written
by Marlene's elder sister, Anneli, and its sequel
"Carpe Diem", this work stands in stark contrast partly
owing to the age gap between the two girls, but above
all because of their dramatically different characters.

Marlene Yeo

Skating at the
Edge of the Wood

Note on layout
Much of this book was composed based on letters written by Marlene to her cousin Jutta, which Jutta kept. The "For Jutta" chapters consist primarily of these contemporaneous descriptions, augmented by post-war notes: the two are distinguished by the use of contrasting typefaces.

Skating at the Edge of the Wood
by Marlene Yeo

Published by Ōzaru Books, an imprint of BJ Translations Ltd
Street Acre, Shuart Lane, St Nicholas-at-Wade,
BIRCHINGTON, CT7 0NG, U.K.
www.ozaru.net

First edition published 8 March 2015
Printed by Lightning Source
ISBN: 978-0-9931587-2-8

Contents

About suffering they were never wrong,
The Old Masters: how well they understood
Its human position; how it takes place
While someone else is eating or opening a window or just walking dully along;
How, when the aged are reverently, passionately waiting
For the miraculous birth, there always must be
Children who did not specially want it to happen, skating
On a pond at the edge of a wood:
They never forgot
That even the dreadful martyrdom must run its course
Anyhow in a corner, some untidy spot
Where the dogs go on with their doggy life and the torturer's horse
Scratches its innocent behind on a tree

from Musée des Beaux Arts
W.H. Auden

I. MICKELAU - SUMMER 1944

"Do you think any of us will still be alive this time next year?" Anneli's voice sounded matter-of-fact; her face, in the late evening twilight, looked expressionless.

I felt as though my inside turned hollow and I couldn't breathe. Whatever had prompted my sister's remark, at this of all times?

Anneli, Marlene, Mutti and Väti in the conservatory

It was a peaceful summer evening. We were sitting at the table in the conservatory. Supper had been cleared away some time ago. Fräulein Genzer, the cook, had gone back to the kitchen. The two agricultural apprentices and the farm secretary, who shared their meals with us, had gone to their rooms. The rest of us – my father, my mother, my sister Anneli, my cousin Jutta Kowalewski and I – had stayed in our places. We always sat like this in the dusk, without candles or paraffin lamps, partly because of the blackout regulations, but mostly because we liked it that way. The strong scent of mignonettes came through the open windows, justifying their rather insignificant daytime existence. And on the wireless – I remember it clearly – they were playing "Tales from the Vienna Woods".

The moment has stayed in my memory as the exact point when the war started to threaten **me**: would **I** be alive this time next year?

It was July 1944. I was thirteen years old. Already the Second World War had gone on for nearly five years, but it had had little impact on my childhood in Mickelau, a farm near the Russian border of East Prussia.

Mutti with her children – 1931

The boss some feared, some respected

Väti with his children outside the new conservatory – 1939

Panoramic view of farmyard from house

East Prussia was a special place, both because of its geographical position and its history. On the pre-war maps of Europe, which was all I ever saw at home and in the village school, it looked like a mere apostrophe to Germany, part of the Reich by virtue of its colour, but separated from it by the "Polish corridor". Its population was equally ambiguous: it consisted of the descendants of native Slavs and of German settlers who moved east after the colonization by the Teutonic Knights in the 15th century; as well as of immigrants from neighbouring Poland and the Baltic States, and of indeterminate mixtures of all these. People's national allegiances varied accordingly. But I think the majority felt themselves to be first and foremost East Prussians, although there was no such country.

During the summer of 1939, there were several military manoeuvres in our neighbourhood. Once, my father took me to see one. I found it quite exciting, rather like a motorized point-to-point, but I hated the monstrous, noisy tanks and the way in which they churned up good farming land.

Rear approach to the farm (Summer 1944) **Rear approach to the farm (Winter 1944)**

On 1 September, I found my mother crying when I woke up: German troops had invaded Poland during the night. I suddenly felt threatened in my childhood happiness, more by the unaccustomed experience of seeing her so openly and inconsolably in tears than by the events that had provoked this. When Britain and France declared war on Germany two days later, it meant little to me. These countries were so remote that they might as well have been on another planet. And so, as far as I was concerned, life went on as before.

Like most of the big farms in East Prussia at the time, our 333 hectares of land consisted of a mixture of arable and pasture. We kept and bred horses – mostly Trakehner, the East Prussian breed that had won international fame in show jumping and dressage. In 1940 we had bought our own stallion, "Illyrier", for a very reasonable price – or so my father thought until he discovered his quirk: he only served virgins, and so had to be tricked into mating with any of the older mares.

One of the advantages of the Trakehner breed was that, although they were elegant riding horses, they were also strong enough for farm work. In addition, we had about 20 heavier carthorses, though none, I think, that didn't have some Trakehner blood in them.

First day on the pony, admired by Opa and Oma Wiemer, Mutti and her cousin Eka

Early teens, riding Loki

We also bred Friesian cattle, and one of the earliest tasks that I enjoyed doing for my father was to fill in the exact marking of a cow on a blank outline picture, for registration with the stud book. The patch at the tail end had to be black, otherwise the poor beast was condemned as unfit for a pedigree herd, and had to be sold. It struck me as a very unfair system of judging quality.

We bred pigs and sheep and all kinds of poultry: turkeys, geese, ducks, hens – Leghorns and Rhode Island Reds – and even a few guinea fowl that flew high into the branches of the birch tree by the bull shed and startled visitors with their screeches. All this livestock kept us self-sufficient and to spare, in meat, eggs, milk and, until the introduction of rationing made this illegal, home-made butter. We grew all our own feedstuffs: oats, barley, mangel-wurzels and swedes; and human food too: rye, wheat, potatoes and, in the garden, all the vegetables and fruit to see us through from one year to the next.

The war had brought about a few changes in the population of Mickelau. Although my father was exempt from military service as a farmer, some of the farm hands had become soldiers and reappeared only occasionally, looking thoroughly unfamiliar in their uniforms. But it had always been the old men who were my friends, and most of them were still about: old Schwarz, the pigman, smelling of pigswill and chew; Kowalies, the shepherd, with one sleeve of his jacket pinned up with a safety-pin because there was no arm to fill it. He sometimes spoke to the sheep and heifers in his native Lithuanian, making it sound like magic incantations. He was now described as "stateless", and although I didn't understand what it meant, I felt sorry for him.

And there was Schalonka, with his bushy moustache, who was in charge of a team of working horses. He had let me ride in the saddle in front of him when I could barely walk, and, a year ago, had taught me to control his team of four single-handed and even to ride them into the pond to drink after a day's work.

New faces appeared at the farm. They marked the different stages of the war for me. The German occupation of Poland brought the Biernacki family to us, as part of the so-called resettlement of Poles with German connections. Frau Biernacki looked like a witch: a sallow face surrounded by untidy blackish hair. She was a specialist on fungi and tried to convert us to eating a kind of boletus that turned a lurid purple when bruised. Her husband was very sinister looking too. Both were the most unlikely parents of their beautiful daughter Halina, who had very thick flaxen plaits and a skin so white it was almost transparent.

At around the same time, a group of old men from White Russia (Belarus) came to work on the farm. This had something to do with a special deal struck between the German and Soviet governments who were then on the same side of the war. I liked them because they spoke funny broken German and fussed over me in much the same way as our resident farm hands.

Lunchtime: forced labour from White Russia

A party of Belgian and French prisoners-of-war joined the Mickelau work force in the summer of 1941. Their presence was to me the only manifestation of the war on the Western Front. They impressed me with their ability to speak fluent French, and embarrassed me by their assumption that I could, too. This left me tongue-tied and reluctant to have much to do with them. Anneli, on the other hand, specialized in friendships and even clandestine flirtations with them: French was one of the subjects she was studying at University, and this gave her a secret language in front of the maids in the kitchen, where most of the conversation took place.

Like all the local farm hands, the prisoners lived in the tied cottages in the valley below the farmyard. The difference was that the native labourers led self-contained lives, each family with their own front door. They had their own plots of land for growing vegetables, and a shared outhouse for keeping their own pigs, cows and poultry. Part of their wages consisted of a *deputat*[1].

The Belgians, on the other hand, depended on their weekly food rations which they had to fetch from our house. They were entitled to the same rations as the German residents, and my mother meticulously doled out the correct amount.

---

[1] feedstuffs for their livestock

In 1942, two pretty Ukrainian girls, Hela and Katya, came to us as so-called voluntary landgirls, but they never made any secret of the fact that they had been deported against their will. By then, Germany and the Soviet Union were at war against each other, and the German army had conquered large parts of Russia. The girls were taken from their homes, ostensibly to do a day's work for the occupation forces, but instead, they had been transported straight to East Prussia, without so much as a good-bye to their families.

Hela and Katya, forced labour from Ukraine

Hela – with her blond hair and blue eyes – would have passed for German, had it not been for her high Slav cheekbones. Katya, on the other hand, was a picture book Russian: jet black hair encircled her round face with unruly ringlets, her cheeks were like polished apples, and her dark, almost black, eyes sparkled with cheerfulness or anger, and misted over with melancholy in quick succession. At sixteen and seventeen, the girls were still just close enough to me in age to become proper friends, with all the ups and downs of friendship. They taught me many Russian phrases, proverbs and songs, and I was very eager to learn, particularly because of my fascination with another group of newcomers to the farm: the Russian prisoners-of-war.

Hela with Nikolai (Soviet POW)

Their very names were like poetry: Vassili, Nikolai, Gregór... They were the only group whose status as prisoners was in any way obvious – a uniformed guard with a gun over his shoulder hovered over at least some of them during the day (as they were split up into different working parties, it could never be all of them) and, after work, they were locked up behind a high wire enclosure which surrounded their living quarters in the oldest farm cottage. Whenever I saw them there, like caged animals, my inside contracted. And when I heard them sing their dark melancholy folk songs, tears came rushing to my eyes. I felt such pity for them, and longed to be accepted by them as a friend. And I fell in love with two of them at once.

I – and, of course, my cousin Jutta. She and I did everything in unison that summer.

By the silver birches

Anneli, Marlene, a friend from Berlin
and Jutta

At the Baltic coast

Claus, Lore Kowalewski, Annelore, Anneli, Frank
Jutta, Rolf, Marlene

Since I had started Secondary School in 1941, I had lived with the Kowalewski family in Insterburg during weekdays in term time. I always hated being away from Mickelau. Sometimes, to console myself, I went to the riding school on the outskirts of the town, just to hang round the loose boxes and absorb the smell of horse. Every weekend, as soon as school finished on a Saturday morning, I went home on the little narrow-gauge railway. This way, I missed the compulsory Saturday afternoon rallies of the Hitler Youth movement, much to the disgust of my uncle Egon who, as a convinced Nazi, thought I had got my priorities wrong. The only thing that made my days in Insterburg bearable was the company of Jutta – but even that was better when she came to Mickelau with me. In the summer of 1944 she spent the whole of the school holidays with us.

Hindenburg Oberschule

Class 3A

Hitler Youth membership card

The Kowalewski family

We enrolled as "casual labour" on the farm and, in spite of my mother's pleading, drove ourselves to the point of exhaustion in an effort to prove that we weren't just the boss's relations playing at farming. At five-thirty in the morning, when Heiland, the foreman, rang the bell at the gable end of the stables, we were in the yard with all the other farm hands, waiting to be allocated our jobs for the day. And when, during the corn harvest, work went on until nightfall, we'd be there with the last load.

Getting to school

Summer – pony and trap

Winter – pony and sledge

Alternate modes of transport

Cycling at the front of the house

Väti's first car, an Opel – summer 1934

Hitching a ride on the liquid manure wagon with Anneli

In the garden

Always happy outdoors

Picking berries together

The greenhouse – peekaboo!

We wielded pitchforks to turn the hay in the meadows, we stooked sheaves of rye and barley, we drove rack wagons along the rows of stooks for loading, or we followed the rack wagons with horse-drawn raking machines, raking up the loose straw that had dropped from the sheaves during loading. We even tried our hand at tying sheaves with a band of straw in the odd-shaped corners of fields where the binder couldn't go; but we were too clumsy and found that our arms wouldn't stretch far enough to encompass a large enough bundle. As for packing the sheaves onto the rack wagons in a straight-sided box-shaped load, nobody wanted to take the responsibility of teaching us: even experts sometimes created a load with a list to one side, which led to its collapse on the way to the farm – an accident that threw out of balance the whole rhythm of empty-wagon-full-wagon, and therefore never failed to provoke my father's unholy wrath.

Fieldwork

Preparing,

turning,

resting,

raking

"Advanced technology" 1940s style – our first automatic binder

Packing sheaves on a rack wagon

With Väti on Varusschlacht – riding before I can walk

Every little thing that interfered with the smooth running of the work led to a furious outburst from my father. He used to ride over the farm on his mount Varusschlacht and, later, her daughter Visitation (all descendants of one mare had to have names beginning with the same initial) to inspect the work in progress. Jutta and I soon learnt to read the signals of his approach: conversations dried up as everybody's efforts intensified – but not always soon enough to escape an angry dressing-down. We worried on the other people's behalf, not on our own. In or out of sight, we never slackened, not only because of the embarrassing consciousness of being the boss's daughter and niece, but even more because we loved the challenge of doing a proper job.

Our customary Sunday afternoon family stroll

Checking the fields and livestock

When the Kowalewskis came, we did it with the pony cart due to Uncle Egon's rheumatism

Jutta's and my main concern each morning was: which of us would be attached to the same working party as Vassili? Vassili was in charge of a team of four pale chestnuts. He would come thundering along the farm tracks with the empty wagon, cracking his whip above the horses' heads louder than anyone else on the farm. His hair matched his horses' manes: pale yellow, straight and dishevelled. He nearly always had a cheerful grin stretching from ear to ear on his broad sunburnt face. To be in the vicinity of that grin was what we longed for.

Or else, to be where Karp would look at us with deep dark soulful eyes. Karp was the complete opposite of Vassili: a frail and melancholy intellectual who was utterly inept at farm work. While Vassili had been given a post of responsibility, my father generally saw to it that Karp did the less strenuous and less skilled jobs where the damage done would be limited.

Feeding the horses with Jutta

Jutta and I could not make up our minds as to which of the two was our favourite. Each appealed to different aspects of our romantic natures. We would never have called it love. That sort of soppy language belonged to the likes of Anneli, Gerda (the pretty, curly-haired farm secretary) and, more recently, Hela the Ukrainian, who had started a deep romance with Nikolai, one of the prisoners. Nevertheless, we were happy enough to be teased about it – especially by my mother, who was a useful accomplice.

Prisoners who came to the kitchen on errands hardly ever left empty-handed. But I think Karp aroused my mother's protective instincts more than most, and if Jutta or I were within reach, she would let us take the credit. She would give us a chunk of black pudding, a slice of smoked ham, or a yeast bun for quick transfer from our pocket to his. The fact that the whole operation had to happen fast and secretively only added to its attraction in our eyes. Although the maids themselves were not above a few friendships and flirtations of their own, we could never be sure that they wouldn't inform against us if ever they had a grudge against their employers.

Befriending prisoners-of-war was a crime punishable by imprisonment. Advertising hoardings in Insterburg were full of posters proclaiming that "anyone who treats prisoners of war like Germans becomes a traitor to the German people. It is forbidden to talk to prisoners-of-war of any country, or to Poles or workers from the east... Once an enemy, always an enemy!"

I had become totally confused about the concept "enemy". The Poles of my childhood had not been the enemy, but Poland after September 1939 was; the Biernackis were not... or were they?

The Soviet Union was full of communists who were the enemy; but somehow, during the first two years of the war, they had been allies. Now they were the arch-enemy, far worse than the warmongering British under the evil Churchill who were, in spite of all, supposed to be more "like us". But I could see with my own eyes that the Soviet prisoners were just like us!

The corn harvest: men mow, women bind

Nearly ready

Schalonka and Frau Schalonka

Ivan (Soviet POW), Hilde (maid), Hela   Hela, Gregór (Soviet POW), Frau Haupt

As the summer wore on, a new sound mingled with the usual farm noises: a low rumbling, like distant thunder. Vassili, grinning, would hold up his finger and say, "Russki coming!" and we'd all roar with laughter. Jutta and I made up songs of many verses with the refrain, "Crash, bang, tralala, the Russian army isn't far."

It wasn't only the noise that made one think of an approaching thunderstorm: there was also the same sense of urgency. Just as when the harvest was threatened by a sudden downpour, the horses were urged into a trot with the full load of corn on the rack wagons, and sometimes even into a gallop on the way back to the fields with the empty wagons. This was against all the rules I'd been taught, and it made me angry on behalf of the horses. However, the people, too, worked flat out, with sweat pouring down their faces.

There had been an official appeal to the farmers in the rich agricultural areas to speed up the harvest. The towns of the Reich depended on East Prussian food supplies. (The appeal did not mention fear about the crops falling into enemy hands.) My father didn't need such prompting. I think he reacted instinctively to anything that threatened a safe harvest home, be it conquering hordes or bad weather.

But thunderstorms were enjoyable. When the storm broke, we'd sit in the comfortable shelter of the conservatory and watch the lightning. There was so much sky in our flat open landscape. When I was small, I often used to change into my bathing suit as soon as the worst of the storm was over, and run about in the rain, letting the mud squelch between my bare toes. I'd breathe in great gulps of damp, earthy air. And when I came in, my mother would rub me down like a sweaty horse.

I was never afraid of thunderstorms. And in this, the rumble of gunfire was very different; for although we would joke about it, I certainly was afraid. And when I lay in bed at night, Anneli's question kept repeating itself more insistently in my mind: would we be alive this time next year?

One night we were woken by loud explosions. From our drive, we watched an eerie firework display: clusters of bright white balls hung among the stars (a device used by enemy aircraft to light up an area to be bombed, sacrilegiously nicknamed "Christmas trees"); a criss-cross pattern of searchlights and tracer-fire and, lower down on the horizon, an overall red glow.

"An air raid – must be over Gumbinnen," my father said firmly.

"But I thought that was the direction of Ins..." I started. A kick in the shins from Anneli, with a sideways glance at Jutta, silenced me. Jutta's family was, of course, in Insterburg.

"As though I was stupid enough to be fooled!" Jutta said to me later.

Not much harm was done by the bombing of Insterburg that time – and, from Jutta's and my point of view, some good: for the start of the new school term was postponed indefinitely, and so we could both stay where we were. It never occurred to me to question whether Jutta's delight was genuine. It was, after all, self-evident that life in Mickelau was better than life in Insterburg in every way.

II. MICKELAU - AUTUMN 1944

The summer seemed to go on forever that year, belying the feeling of impermanence that the background sounds of war engendered. The corn harvest was finished in record time. The barn was bulging with a bumper crop of rye, wheat and barley waiting to be threshed. We had made a start on the potatoes, and still the heat wave continued.

Jutta and I enjoyed even this most unpopular, backbreaking job – potato picking. A horse-drawn machine went along the furrows, digging up and scattering the potatoes, which then had to be gathered in heavy willow baskets and tipped into strategically placed sacks. If we worked fast enough, we might have a chance to help the amateur Karp clear the strip allocated to him!

Although we tried to ignore the gunfire, a new set of arrivals on the farm brought home to us the fact that Germany was losing the war. One afternoon, a pathetic party trundled into the yard. It looked like an illustration in a sad Russian fairy tale: a two-wheeled cart pulled by a shaggy pony under a high curved wooden yoke; in it, an old man with a flowing white beard, and a small round-faced boy. A young man with sleek black hair and solemn, unapproachable face was walking alongside it. This was the Mosin family – grandfather, father and son; and they were Russian refugees.

Mosin family, refugees from partisans in German-occupied Russia

(Volodya, Vitya, "Opa")

By 1943, German troops had overrun most of the European parts of the Soviet Union, as far as the outskirts of Leningrad in the north and Stalingrad in the south. Because of their brutal treatment of the civilian population, a strong resistance movement developed in the occupied territories. The so-called partisans fought, not only against the Germans, but also against Russians who in any way collaborated with the conquerors. The women in the Mosin household had washed a German soldier's clothes, and so they, together with four children, were massacred. The rest of the family escaped by a mere accident. Since then, they had depended on the Germans for protection. When the German army began

17

to retreat, therefore, the Mosins, too, took to the road. By the time they arrived in Mickelau, they had been travelling for a whole year.

While the grandfather (whom we called "Opa") and his son Volodya worked on the farm, Anneli took care of three-year-old Vitya. He soon called her his "Mama". He was a cheerful, affectionate child, and only occasionally did we catch a glimpse of his traumatic past: he used to tease us by throwing himself down, all floppy and lifeless, on the floor, saying, *Kapuuut!*[2] If he was in the garden when a plane flew over, he would throw himself headlong under the nearest shrub for cover.

And then an artillery unit of the German army was billeted in our district. Major Damm and his orderly, his groom and two horses, plus a driver and car, were stationed with us and served as an excuse for various junior officers to pay us visits from neighbouring farms. Among the most regular were lieutenants Caspari and Meiwes, both in undisguised competition for Anneli's favours. Their visits continued even after Major Damm had been posted to the front and, within days, killed.

Mickelau was like the stage in a play where you can tell the end is near by the number of actors crowding in for the final scene; and the background of gunfire was like dramatic sound effects. My brother Claus, who had had to join the army in December 1943, on his 17th birthday, unexpectedly came home on leave. Anneli did not go back to University for the new term. Instead, she arranged a string of dinner parties and dances as though they all had to be fitted in before the final curtain.

Party time – that meant a transformation of house and inhabitants to unaccustomed splendour. As far as the house was concerned, I thoroughly approved.

In party gear – 1939

It was only on special occasions that we used the drawing room: its stiff, twirly mahogany furniture did not invite people to flop down, harvest-weary, in dusty breeches and fruit-stained cotton skirts; but it was just the right setting for beautifully turned-out ladies in evening dress sipping their after-dinner coffee

---

[2] (kaputt) – "I'm done in!"

from tiny Meissen cups. On such evenings, my father lit the paraffin pressure lamp that hung from the centre of the ceiling. It was a complicated ceremony, and the moment when the fragile gauze mantle burst, with a pop, into brilliant white light, was almost as magical as the first sight of the candle-lit fir tree on Christmas Eve: suddenly, the whole tall big room was illuminated, right to the corner where the glass cabinet displayed crystal bowls and hand-painted china.

There was a similar ceiling light in the sitting room, where it completely changed those familiar surroundings from their usual cosy atmosphere to one of forbidding grandeur. On ordinary winter evenings, a table lamp with a plain brass belly and a milky porcelain shade cast a warm circle of light on to the wool-embroidered "kelim" table cloth; it seemed to hold us together, all of us who sat round its circumference, reading, knitting, playing rummy or just talking. The rest of the room was then full of familiar and yet mysterious shadows.

On party days, the brightness of the hissing pressure lamp drove out those shadows, and the place became a men's room, the "Herrenzimmer". The air smelt of Schnaps and wine and cigar smoke; the grey marble ashtray, almost too heavy for me to lift, filled with the stubs of cigars and gold-edged cigarettes. The deep club armchairs fitted comfortably round the well-covered figures of gentlemen farmers and army officers. I could hardly believe then that, on many occasions, they had served my imagination as coach-and-two and been driven at a gallop across the East Prussian plains.

In the dining room extra leaves were fitted into the table, extending it from its minimal circle seating eight to a large oval with space for about 24 place settings. Cut glass, silver cutlery, and starched white table napkins big enough for tablecloths gleamed in candlelight. Both Frieda and Hilde, the maids, served at table, dolled up in shiny black frocks and white aprons. And I was, at such times, scolded for stacking the empty plates, rather than being rebuked for "not lifting a finger to help".

Fräulein Genzer, the cook, did not eat with us on those occasions. She flapped around the kitchen in a terrible temper, looking like Rumpelstilzken, with her frizzy grey hair sticking out all round her cross and flustered face. And I could imagine her, like Rumpelstilzken, tearing herself apart in a fit of anger.

Anneli looked lovely when she dressed up. Her newly washed dark blond hair fell in gentle waves down to her shoulders and was my great envy, as my own yellow strands always hung straight as straw. Sometimes she wore lipstick, much to my disgust – though I had to admit it gave her a kind of daring beauty. No wonder all the men round about fell for her.

As for my mother, I wasn't so sure: the way I loved her best was in her everyday cotton frocks and half-aprons, with her brown hair arranged in a slightly dishevelled roll in the nape of her neck. Before a party, she went through an elaborate procedure with a pair of iron tongs which were heated over a special spirit burner. She put her hair between the two blades, strand by strand, pulled a little lever, and in this way gradually covered her head with tight wavy lines. It made her look a stranger and, I thought, behave like a stranger too, so that I hardly dared touch her, much though I liked to stroke the slightly bobbly material of her navy blue silk dress which had buttons that glittered like diamonds.

But my father, above all, looked wrong when he exchanged his everyday riding breeches and check jacket for a dark three-piece suit, and his ordinary fob watch for the slim gold version. I understood then why people were frightened of him – he looked formidable even to me.

Jutta and I enjoyed the party preparations. Under Anneli's instructions, we made table decorations from conkers and red and golden autumn leaves. We helped devise place cards in anagrams, puzzles and verses. We also enjoyed the food, especially if the sweet was ice cream. This was a very rare treat, as it involved a complicated operation: a mixture of whipped cream and eggs and fruit was spooned into a metal bowl with a tight-fitting lid, which was then buried under chips of ice in the coldest part of the ice-cupboard. The ice itself had been harvested from the pond in winter: men with special ice saws cut large blocks of it to be stored in the ice-house under layers of straw and earth.

After the meal, Jutta and I usually escaped to the kitchen. By then Fräulein Genzer would have calmed down, and there would be a boisterous party atmosphere among the kitchen staff. Sometimes Auguste was summoned from the farm cottages to give a hand with the washing up. This had to be done in white enamel bowls on the kitchen table, with water heated in saucepans on the range. Auguste had one of those tremulous operatic sopranos that made Jutta and me cringe. *"Oh wie wuppert, wie wuppert, wie wuppert mir mein Herz / Vor lauter Lieb und Schmerz..."*[3] she used to trill. And we would hide our giggles behind the nearest cupboard door.

Anneli always wanted people to dance at her parties. The carpet would be rolled up, and the wind-up gramophone would blare out, not just Strauss waltzes and tangos, but also the very latest in foxtrots and quicksteps and – my favourite – the Lambeth Walk. The snag was that, with all the officers about, there was an acute shortage of females. There were Anneli and Gerda, and occasionally an ex-schoolfriend of Anneli's who'd come and stay the night. But most of Anneli's current friends lived too far away – in Hamburg, Vienna and the Rhineland.

So Jutta and I were dragooned into joining the party in the drawing room. We weren't much good: we sat awkwardly against the wall on stiff upright chairs, and talked in whispers about what Karp would make of it all if he saw us, and if, after the war, we'd invite him to such occasions. Or we'd dance, the two of us together, and briefly enjoy ourselves. But to be asked to dance by one of the officers used to embarrass us terribly. Jutta in particular would blush crimson whenever Caspari led her to the floor. So much so that I began to wonder if, not content with her parallel affections for Karp and Vassili, she also had a crush on Anneli's most ardent admirer.

She was not given time to come into conflicts about this: her father, Egon Kowalewski, rang up to call her back, as the town of Insterburg was to be evacuated to Saxony. So on 20 October, she and I were separated for the first time in nearly four months.

Two days later, my own life in Mickelau came to an end.

---

[3] "Oh how my heart's a-trembling with so much love and pain..."

III. FOR JUTTA - 22 OCTOBER 1944

Jutta, how I miss you. I never thought that you and I would cry when it came to parting – we who pride ourselves on being so unsentimental! I'm glad they let me take you to the station on my own. The clip clopping of the pony's hooves was quite comforting on the way back, and that scratching sound on the front wheel of the pony trap gave me something to think about. I meant to tell Väti about it, but with all the upheaval of preparing for our escape, I forgot. Not that it mattered: all the coaches and carts were oiled and overhauled before we set out.

I'm so used to sharing my experiences with you that ever since you left I've kept a sort of running commentary in my head for you. Will we ever meet again so that we can actually talk about it all?

When I had seen you off, I just wanted to be left alone to be miserable. I reversed the trap into the shed, unharnessed the pony and then stayed with her in the stable. Oh the comfort of putting your head against a horse's neck and breathing warm horsy smells...

But everything was abnormal. Instead of the labourers being busy in the fields, ploughing, and harvesting mangel-wurzels, they were rushing around the farmyard, in and out of stables and sheds. Whenever they came upon me, they made jolly remarks, and I wasn't at all in the mood for that. So I fled to my hideout in the lovely linden tree at the bottom of the orchard. Ridiculous! Most of the leaves had already dropped, and I must have been as conspicuous in its branches as in a rookery in midwinter.

The house, then. There was pandemonium: cardboard boxes and newspapers and piles of stuff for packing in each room; saucepans and other cooking utensils in the kitchen; china in the dining room; bedding and clothes in my parents' bedroom...

I tried to become invisible in my room. You would have laughed to see me there, cowering on the bed, close to the wardrobe, with Rommel, Dönitz and Galland[4] sternly looking down at me from their fancy home-made frames. Remember shovelling Galland out of a snowdrift on the road to Trempen last winter? The thrill of recognizing him! I've changed a lot since then, though I hardly dare admit it even to myself. Is it because of our friendship with the Russian prisoners? I catch myself thinking that maybe it isn't all that admirable to get medals for killing lots of people... All my elaborate scrapbooks of generals and colonels with their Teutonic crosses with diamonds and swords and whatnots[5]: it made me laugh, suddenly, to see them stacked among the even more elaborate volumes of dog and horse pictures and sketches for my future kennels and studs! I want to take them all to safety, but I wonder if the hero pictures might get me into trouble if the Russian army catches up with us. I wish you and I had discussed this before you left. It's no use asking Anneli for advice: she'd only

---

[4] Rommel, Dönitz and Galland were German war heroes
[5] military medals

make snooty remarks about our collection, while she herself wastes her own time on soppy pictures of film stars... And Mutti? I know what she'd say: "Don't even think about getting caught; it won't happen..." But I know she would only pretend to feel confident in order to cheer me up.

She soon rooted me out from my hiding place and told me to help pack eggs; less because she needed my help, I think, than because she wanted to cajole me out of my melancholy.

Actually, it was good fun packing eggs: a quarter page of newspaper wrapped round each egg, twisted up at the ends like a New Year cracker. Although I'd often collected eggs from the chicken house, I had no idea just how quickly they accumulated if you didn't sell any: there were hundreds of them! Vassili, of all people, was detailed to help me. How romantic, I hear you say! I could easily have fulfilled my promise to say good-bye to him from you. Sorry – I just couldn't get the words out. I also wanted somehow to apologize to him for running away from his fellow countrymen, and to tell him how pleased I was for him and the other prisoners: soon they'd be free... But he looked oddly miserable himself – and you know how he usually grins all over his face. Maybe he is pining for you?! Mutti says that for all of them it's a case of "from the frying pan into the fire", and who wouldn't rather be a prisoner in Mickelau than a soldier at the front?

Later, Mutti sent me to the loft to fetch jam. Not, as in the past, a bowlful scooped out of the big earthenware pots for immediate use, but the pots themselves, three of them, tied down with greaseproof paper and labelled in Mutti's neat small handwriting: morello cherry, raspberry, redcurrant jelly. So there wasn't any scope for the habitual private feast under the slanting roof. Remember how Mutti used to insist, with forethought, that we took a separate little bowl and spoon so that we didn't make the whole pot go mouldy with our spit? I carried the pots down those steep creaking stairs to the first floor, one pot at a time, scared stiff that I might drop it through the gaps in the rickety banisters. When I was small, I was terrified of falling through those gaps myself, and of landing with a broken neck outside Fräulein Genzer's door. How long ago that seems now!

I feel quite old all at once. I walk around, like someone under sentence of death, remembering all my long past. When I was in the loft, I peeped through the slatted door of the leather store opposite the jam store, and was suddenly on a sleigh ride... All because of the smell of oiled leather and the sight of the bell harness hanging from a nail under the rafters. Most of the spare harnesses had been fetched down for use during the trek. But I suppose it makes sense to leave the bells: the days of sleigh rides with the neighbours are over.

Magic mornings of hoarfrost on birch trees and fences, of blinding white carpets of snow and glassy skies, so beautiful that I had to hold my breath. Then we pestered Väti until he agreed: no job was important enough to waste such a day. He rang round the other big farmers close by – the Bagdahns, the Kuhns, the Müllers: "Coming for a sleigh ride?" The best sleigh was spruced up and decked out with horsehair cushions and sheepskin rugs that you sat in like in a sack, up to your waist, and that still had a whiff of sheep pen about them. The leather cover that buttoned against the sides of the sleigh all round your feet was newly oiled, and so was the harness with its strips of tiny brass bells.

Which way is the slope?

On those occasions, I didn't mind being muffled up in layers of sweaters and shawls and hat and gloves and mittens and several pairs of woollen stockings and socks in lace-up boots. I didn't even mind having the exposed parts of my face plastered with a covering of Nivea cream.

Going for a walk after the thaw

Otto, the coachman – resplendent on the box, in silky black fur hat and cape that gradually turned to polar bear where his breath frosted over – reeked of mothballs. He held the reins in one of his cloven-hoof driving mittens, and the whip in the other. The mares' buttocks gleamed like shiny silk. Such stillness! Silence made audible in the tinkle of sleigh bells, and made visible in whiteness. That's how I still think of it.

We'd stop for lunch at some pub or other: pea soup and sausages, or ghastly *Königsberger Fleck*[6], the very sight of which turned my stomach, with its slimy bits of tripe swimming in what looked like grey washing-up water. But there was also the treat of delicious baker-made crusty rolls – a change from our home baked rye bread. That was the only good part of the lunch break, as far as I was concerned. It was boring when there were no other children, and it was embarrassing when there were: what had I to say to Evchen Lau? My only friends in Mickelau (when Jutta wasn't there) were Irene, the shepherd's daughter, and Ursel, the dairyman's daughter, and they never got invited on those outings. Well, they would have felt out of place, I can see that: without proper table manners, and only speaking Plattdeutsch.

The grown-ups had a boisterous time over their lunch. They gradually disappeared in a fog of cigar smoke, drinking grog, talking and shrieking with laughter. Sometimes I wondered whether that, to them, was the best part of the sleigh outings.

Not that I minded delay in going home until after dark. The flickering coach lamps on either side of the sleigh turned Otto into a black cardboard cut-out. And they illuminated the mares' buttocks as if for a flashlight photograph of steaming horse apples that dropped every so often from under the gracefully curled up tails. The delicious smell of it, in the sharp winter air! I used to want to bottle it and sell it as horse-shit perfume.

Most times, when we travelled at night, I slipped right down between my parents' feet into the sheepskin rug, where the smell of mothballs lingered. Only my face stuck out at the top, for stargazing under Mutti's direction.

In all the commotion of packing, one thing happened that would have made you laugh. As you know, in August Mutti had sent our most precious things to Onkel Rudi in Dresden for safe keeping. But she hadn't sent our best dinner service for fear that it might get smashed in the post. Now she didn't think it was suitable picnic ware for refugees. So she carefully wrapped it in layers of newspaper and piled it into cardboard boxes. When it grew dark, she and Nikolai sneaked into the back garden to bury it. Why Nikolai? Maybe she means him to have it? I haven't a clue, and I didn't bother asking. She would have said it's for when we come back after the war... Anyway, it didn't matter: when she stamped on her newly dug mound of earth to firm it, she heard horrible crunching sounds of breaking china! Can't you just imagine a hopeful treasure hunter coming upon boxes full of broken bits! Needless to say, Mutti didn't see the funny side of it.

Earlier in the day, there was a telephone request for help from Kowarren, where the authorities have set up a soup kitchen for refugees. Mutti and Hilde went there with the pony trap full of vegetables and meat, to cook them a meal. Apparently the refugees had left their homes in such a hurry that they didn't even pack a day's provisions.

---

[6] tripe stew, an East Prussian speciality

Later that evening, they arrived on the farm too: hundreds of wagons covered more or less securely with tarpaulins like the ones we put on top of hayricks. The farmyard looked like a scene from those colonization-of-Africa films. People were milling around all over the place, like ants when you disturb an anthill. Even our drawing room was turned into a dormitory. But the refugees weren't a bit grateful. If anything, they seemed to resent the fact that we still had things to give them. Tarred with the Communist brush, was how Väti described them. But what are they running away from, in that case? Aren't the Russians their friends? We watched them suspiciously when they left early next morning, in case they loaded up some of our ready-packed belongings.

As soon as they had gone, the Russian prisoners got our own wagons ready for our evacuation. A bit ironic, that, getting the prisoners to do it! But all the other men were busy with their own possessions. Rack wagons, box carts, rubber-carts (or should I call them "plateau wagons" which, Mutti says, is the proper name for the carts with pneumatic tyres), coaches, and even the pony trap – everything is going to be used between us. The labourers' families, the Poles and Ukrainians, and the Belgian prisoners-of-war are all coming on the trek.

The artillery fire still rumbles on continuously, coming closer and closer. Every so often, there's a really loud bang that makes the zinc footbath on the kitchen wall tremble (remember how it came crashing down that year when lightning split the birch tree by the bull shed?). Väti calls them "Big Bertha", whatever that may mean.

Väti spent most of the morning yanking the handle of the telephone until it nearly came off. Half the time the exchange didn't even answer – I suppose because they were bogged down with other people doing exactly the same. When Väti did get through to the various officials whom he tried to contact, they all contradicted each other, and even themselves at different times: "Don't be so alarmist, our army will beat the enemy back..." one minute; then, "Evacuation orders will be issued any time now..." Väti got more and more bad-tempered, and everyone (except me, as usual) kept out of his way.

When he got through to the neighbouring farms, he discovered that some of them had already sent all women and children off by train; others were, like us, waiting for official orders. Can you believe it: it is actually forbidden to leave without these orders, and you can be had for desertion!

On the other hand, there were phone calls from Caspari and Meiwes and several of the other boyfriends Anneli has acquired among the army officers roundabout. "What? Are you still there?!" they asked, with a suggestive pause. Eventually, Caspari came cycling over to tell us what he didn't dare say over the phone: the Russian army is already on East Prussian soil; they have broken through German defences near Eydkau, and Caspari doesn't think there's much chance of stopping them. So he advised us to leave at once.

Väti sent me back and forth with messages to the labourers' cottages all afternoon. "Tell them we're waiting for..." "Tell them to be ready by..." "Tell them to check that..."

I managed to walk past Karp several times, but do you think I gave him your love? Not I. Again the words stuck in my throat. All we did was exchange deep meaningful glances... How you would have laughed!

At the cottages, I found the women busy in their communal back yard, slaughtering geese. Feathers flew about like a blizzard. But even in their hurry, the women separated out the coarse feathers from the down in different pillowcases, as in normal times. What are they going to do with them? Take them on the trek, or leave them for someone else (who?) to stuff their feather beds?

Poor geese. Well, anyway, they would have been killed for Christmas. And at least they escaped the possible ordeal of force-feeding to fatten them up. Mutti says the labourers still do that, in spite of Hitler's law against cruelty to animals. We don't, because of the risk of being reported, not out of pity for the geese! But the memory is still with me: ghastly smell of finger-sized pellets of damp mesh drying on large trays in the kitchen; ghastlier sight of geese held in the vice of Hilde's arm while Frieda and Mutti shoved pellets down their unwilling beaks....

In all the commotion, the women listened to me with such deference, it made me feel quite uncomfortable: I don't want this sense of authority. I don't want to be "the boss's daughter"! I want to dance the polka with Schalonka!

Frieda's wedding to Richard Siemanowski, the dairyman – what a celebration that had been! The Schalonkas' parlour at the back of their house was a tiny room, and when our family crowded into it (we all sat squashed together on the sofa, me on Mutti's lap) there was hardly any room for the other wedding guests. On the table, plates of all the tasty East Prussian specialities – Fladen, Glumsekuchen, Mohnstriezel, S-Kuchen and even Baumkuchen – overlapped like building bricks. You could only see the tablecloth where it hung over the sides: embroidered posies of flowers in red, purple and pink chain stitch, with turquoise and emerald leaves, and little knots of bright yellow pollen in the centres – much more beautiful than any of the ones at home in their tastefully muted beiges and browns, or shades of blue.

Wives and children of resident farm workers

Frieda in the foreground

There was raspberry juice for me to drink out of a glass decorated with bright blobs of colour. I was sweating in my prickly pink organdie frock; for, of course, I had had to dress up. I had submitted to the ordeal more willingly than at other times, for Mutti had impressed upon me the importance of showing respect for the occasion.

Frieda and Richard opened the ball by dancing a waltz in the kitchen to the sound of a borrowed gramophone. And then old Schalonka asked me to do the polka with him: one two three hop, one two three hop, crashing into the furniture. We left too early, I thought: the fun had hardly begun. But Mutti explained on the way home that our presence had cramped everyone's style – "Listen to them now!" – as the sounds of party cheer drifted after us.

I had cried then, because I was deprived of belonging there.

When I told Väti that the labourers were killing their Christmas geese, he said, "Good idea!" and there and then, told the maids to do the same. So off to the pond we went, Hilde and I, to shoo the ducks and geese off the water. Some job, in the middle of the day, as you can well imagine: it's hard enough at dusk! We had to walk round the pond several times, rope stretched taut between us. But though we steadily flipped the water surface with the string, there was always one rebel that suddenly fluttered across, and then the whole flock followed suite, squawking like mad. I think they knew what lay in store for them!

Not content with the duck massacre, Väti asked the guard of the Russian prisoners (who is a butcher by civilian profession) to kill a pig, and to hell with the rationing regulations. I rushed to the furthest corner of the loft and blocked up my ears, so as not to hear the agonized squeals. When I re-emerged, there were duck feathers and pig's blood and gory carcasses all over the place. I thought the grown-ups had gone completely mad, and I longed for your sane company!

Well, I left them to their lunacies and went to sleep on Väti's bedstead, rolled up in various overcoats (all the bedding, even the horsehair mattress, had already been packed). Off and on, I was conscious of a lot of noise, even laughter, from the sitting room. I wondered whether I was missing a party. I wouldn't have put it past Anneli... Once I heard Väti grumble, "I'm not going back in there, if Caspari and Anneli sit on the sofa like that!" and Mutti replying something about them being "engaged". That sounds interesting, I thought, and planned to get up.

But the next thing I knew, it was morning. The goose plucking was still in full swing, and the artillery fire louder than ever. "Get ready to leave, marching orders will be issued in a moment," Väti was told over the telephone. So the horses were harnessed, and our trek lined up.

"Marching orders" was a bit of a misnomer for our conglomeration of vehicles: six wagons drawn by teams of two, a barouche, the pony trap, the Mosins' own panje-cart, a tractor with two trailers, and even the iron-wheeled tractor that we only use on heavy clay! The labourers' families sat perched on top of their own belongings. Claus was riding on "Illyrier". What else can you do with a stallion that isn't broken into harness? Väti and I were to bring up the rear in the car.

27

Claus in riding gear on Illyrier, the stallion

What a strange situation. The Russian prisoners are the only people staying in Mickelau – with their guard, of course. How will the old butcher treat them, when there's nobody to watch over him?! I shudder to think... Väti's idea is that all the men on the trek will come back to Mickelau as soon as they have taken their families and belongings to a safer place. Meanwhile, the Russians will take care of all the livestock. I half expected them to line the road and wave us off, but there was no sign of them. So no farewells at all.

Väti stood by the telephone, expecting final orders from the authorities. In vain.

Eventually, at one o'clock, we stopped waiting and left. The artillery was giving us more than a twenty-one-gun salute, but I wasn't a bit scared. Or miserable. Just numb. All I could think was, Why one o'clock? Why not ten past or half past?

Suddenly there was a strange buzzing sound. I saw Volodya snatch little Vitya from the cart, and in seconds they were both crouching behind a tree. It looked sweet – father and son cuddled together, all among the golden birch leaves. But why?

The buzzing turned to an angry whine. Six planes, one after another, dived down at us, and there was a sharp tak-tak-tak sound, a bit like very quick gun shots at a partridge shoot.

"They're not aiming at us," Väti said – to comfort me, I suppose. Until that moment, the idea had not occurred to me. Then, all at once, I was terrified. But glad, too. It was much easier leaving Mickelau when you were afraid for your life.

IV. FOR JUTTA - 25 OCTOBER 1944

It's amazing how quickly one gets used to the gypsy life. If only you were here with us, we could have some good laughs. Anneli and I do, anyway – off and on. Not during the first two days, though. They were quite horrid.

The roads were cram-full with refugees. It took ages before we got off our drive into the mainstream of traffic. The other refugees were so selfish and wouldn't let us squeeze in; and, when eventually we did, they shouted and yelled at us. Väti says that's how people behave when they are frightened. He told me about himself in the First World War when he was a cavalry officer. They were all galloping like mad, away from a battle. Suddenly the man in front of him crashed to the ground. Väti dug in his spurs and rode on...

I hate that story, but I can't get it out of my mind. I'd rather Väti had been like one of those heroes in the films we used to see at the "Alhambra" in Insterburg, who would have stopped to fling the man across the saddle in front of him at no matter what cost to himself. All the same, I now keep thinking and thinking about what it must have felt like for him.

The trek stops for a rest

You know how we used to joke about the idea of fleeing from the Russians at snail's pace with the iron-wheeled tractor? Well, we'd have been lucky to be able to go that fast! It was all stop and start, stop and start, and standing around for ages, nobody knew why. Once we thought that one of the wagons in front must have broken down. So we pulled off the tarmac onto the cart track alongside, in order to overtake. Too late, we discovered that the end of the stoppage was not even in sight. And suddenly, there was an army truck, trying to go the other way. We had completely blocked the road. As the traffic behind us also stretched on in a seemingly unending line, there was no turning back either.

The soldiers shouted and gesticulated, and the other refugees in their little carts became really abusive: who did we think we were, claiming right of way, did we think we were superior with our tractors and coaches? One of them even lashed out at Claus with a whip. I suppose he did look rather provocative on his beautiful stallion. I wanted to shout back, "Not fair, not fair! We didn't know!" Instead, I just shrank lower under the rugs.

I don't know who had this brainwave: we pulled off the road onto a meadow. There we fed the horses and waited for a chance to thread ourselves back into the queue. Would we be standing there still, I wondered, when the Russian tanks rolled along the road? But towards evening, as various treks stopped for the night, the traffic thinned out. We travelled long after dark to make use of the empty roads. That way, we got ahead of the worst congestion for the following days.

My biggest problem is how to avoid travelling in the same vehicle as Mutti. She is in her worst protective-hen mood towards me, and the idea of enjoying our flight as an adventure doesn't seem to enter her head. Not that I blame her for that; at her age I'd probably be the same. But I want to have some fun!

Anneli and Gerda aren't too bad for company. The trouble with them is they don't know half the folk songs that you and I used to sing. And they certainly can't hold the tune when I sing the descant. Instead they sing those soppy Zarah Leander hits that I can't stand.

Even on the trek, time for a 'picnic'

(Katya, Hela, Marlene, Mutti, Günter, Väti)

The other morning, I was with them and Fräulein Genzer in the barouche. Anneli produced a packet of constipation pills. "Have some," she said, "They taste of chocolate and they have no effect whatsoever." So of course we did, every one of us. Apart from a rather nasty aftertaste they were quite nice and, between us, we finished the packet. By two o'clock, I began to have my suspicions about Anneli's "no effects" guarantee. "You're imagining it!" she said firmly. But by

30

three o'clock I was in no doubt. My own admission was all that the others needed to trigger them off.

What now? Refugee treks as far as the eye could see. We weren't hardened enough to squat in the ditch in full view of the public. Luckily, there was a track leading off into a wood. We urged our horses down this. They were so pleased to be able to stretch their legs after all the slow pace that we thundered along like a Roman chariot in full cry. "What if the others think this is our new route and follow us?" we giggled.

Belgian POWs and Poles on the trek

(Raymond, Lebrun, Vera, *[unidentifiable]*, Fernand, Tadek)

It was lovely in the woods, lonely and peaceful, with lots of inviting little paths for exploring, and good climbing trees, ideal for playing hide-and-seek, if only you'd been there too...

"But how will we find the others again?"

Suddenly, getting back to the main road was even more urgent than our diversion had been. You hear such dreadful stories of people losing each other...

When we were reunited with the rest of our trek, we were so happy, we became quite hysterical for the remaining afternoon. "Look at that woman, hahaha, look at her hat... Look at that name, Gelbsch! Hahaha..." "That's no name for a village," Anneli said dogmatically. She turned to a little old man who was watching our trek from the roadside, his eyes brimming with pity. "Excuse me, what is this place called?" "Yalbsch," he replied in his best East Prussian pronunciation. We doubled up with laughter. I still feel guilty now when I remember the puzzled look on his face.

31

We didn't laugh that evening when we came to the smart estate of Eulenburg-Prassen and asked for accommodation. The farm manager eyed us with obvious disapproval and said there was no room. Only after Väti blew his top did he deign to put us up. You could see his point in a way: a mass bed of straw did not go with the elegant striped wallpaper and brocade curtains. I slept beautifully, though – much more comfortably than on those sprung mattresses in bedsteads without cushioning, from which you get up with a pattern of spirals impressed on your bottom.

All the same, it made us appreciate all the more our lodgings some night later on, on another farm, when we were given two made-up beds with clean sheets. Mutti and I slept in one, Anneli and Vitya in the other. We were even invited to a supper of Klunkermus[7] *and fried tomatoes, at a properly laid table with napkins! Fancy me being impressed by that sort of thing, when all my life I've considered it my biggest treat to be allowed to eat hunks of black bread off the kitchen table with the maids.*

---

[7] hot milk soup with flour dumplings

V. FOR JUTTA - 29 OCTOBER 1944

I've decided to harden myself against farewells. There are so many of them, and Mutti's example is enough to put anybody off: she dissolves into tears just about every morning when we say good-bye to our overnight hosts, even when they've been quite nasty and I, for one, am glad to see the last of them. When they've been kind to us and – as happened once – given us a bag of tomatoes as a parting gift, she just about floods the place.

It's quite strange to watch: one moment she looks normal. Then, suddenly, her face sort of crinkles all over, like a shrivelled seed potato, and there are tears running down all the cracks. I'm still not sure what I'm supposed to do then: look away and pretend I haven't noticed, or try and comfort her... but how? Usually I just hug her and end up crying with her. Very exhausting.

The worst farewell was when Claus left us on 26 October. His official leave had expired six days earlier, on the same day as you left Mickelau, but he had asked the military doctor of the artillery unit if he could give him a certificate of unfitness on some pretext or other. He wrote "sore feet" and gave Claus a week's extension of leave. Luckily nobody thought to examine his certificate or his feet as he was merrily riding along in tight riding boots and all. The unit to which he was told to report is in Saxony (in Chemnitz, to be exact; is that near you?) He is supposed to attend some training course or other. Cushy place, well away from any front, safer than our trek... Which thoughts should have cheered us when we saw him off, but...

You always think it's good-bye forever, but sometimes you're quite soon proved wrong. And then, for one tiny moment, you almost feel cheated because all that heartbreak had been for nothing... No, no, I don't mean that, of course! I want to un-think that thought!

Claus self-conscious in his uniform

The last photo of the Wiemer family

It happened twice with Väti. The first time was on the very day after we left Mickelau. We had spent the night with farmers whom Väti knew. In the morning we listened to their wireless and heard that a "decisive battle" had been won by our troops at Labiau. For one blissful moment I thought this meant we'd all go home, but no, nobody seemed to have much faith in this victory. Only Väti turned back. He was still bothered about our so-called "desertion", because we had left Mickelau without official permission, and so he wanted to show willing. But, I think, more than that, he was worried that Mickelau wasn't properly looked after: Ivan and Vassili would know how to run a farm, but would the guard let them? He's a butcher, for heaven's sake! What does he know about a pedigree herd!

I felt really scared without Väti. I feel safe when he is around, even though I know that doesn't make sense in the present circumstances... At least he knows what to do, and when he gives orders, people take notice of him. When he's away, I keep thinking that I ought to take decisions and be responsible for things, to help Mutti. Anneli manages that, all right – in fact, she seems more in charge of the trek than Mutti – but I'm completely useless at it. So it was a real load off my conscience when he caught up with us again that same evening. He had given up the attempt because the car kept getting bogged down between military vehicles hurrying to the front, and refugee treks hurrying away from it.

Two days later he tried his luck again, not alone this time, but with a car full of people who wanted to go home: Siemanowski, Kowalies, and Frau Schwarz. I would have liked to go, too. Although there was still the continuous rumble of gun fire, it sounded so far away that it wasn't frightening any longer. But Väti said that was probably because we'd travelled away from it, and he'd better go first and make sure.

The rest of us plodded on westwards. On the 28th, we were told about a soup kitchen in Wormditt where we would be able to get a warm meal. Four of us went ahead in the barouche to reconnoitre. Wormditt is a town, but only just. You wouldn't have thought it possible to get lost there. But we did. To start with, we had problems finding the soup kitchen, and when eventually we did, and wanted to guide our trek to it, we couldn't find the trek! It was not until evening that we saw our wagons again, well past Wormditt. They had already moved into night quarters, and there, with them, was... Väti. This time he had been back to Mickelau, and he now had official permission to escort us to our final destination.

Apparently the Russian prisoners are still on the farm. They are harvesting mangel-wurzels, and threshing corn. All of it is immediately transported to the West. What happens to our cattle, what will they eat over the winter? I asked Väti, but he just shrugged.

Väti brought a letter from Nikolai to his beloved girlfriend, Hela. In it he told Hela that when Väti had come back to Mickelau, it had seemed to Nikolai as if his own father had turned up. Apparently all the prisoners are fed up with the lack of order and organization on the farm. As Nikolai had no other present to give to Hela, he sent her a slice of his bread ration. Needless to say, that really opened the floodgates of Mutti's tears.

The whole district of Preussisch Holland has been allocated to refugees from the Angerapp district. We were sent to the village of Ebersbach. There we hung about outside the mayor's office until we were parcelled off to various farms. A bit like the slave trade, I imagine! Our farmer is called Podlech, so is the farmer with whom the Siemanowskis are billeted, **and** the farmer where the Haupts are staying. Half the village seem to be called Podlech, and you give them numbers to differentiate between them. We're with Number One.

It was a ghastly feeling, but Anneli and I didn't have time to be miserable: we both urgently needed a lavatory. So the first thing Anneli asked Mr Podlech No. 1 was where was the loo. He pointed across the yard to a picturesque door with a heart-shaped hole: an outside thunder box! While Anneli hesitated, taken aback by this information, I sprinted off. She followed and gained on me, and we arrived at the door in a dead heat. We jostled to get in. And there, like an answer to a prayer, was a wooden bench with **two** big round holes cut into it. We nearly wet our pants at the last moment, laughing.

I was really grateful for that lavatory. It gave us something to laugh about when we least expected to laugh; and later on, it gave me a place to be alone and cry. There was nowhere else where we could get away from one another.

We were given two small rooms. One had a little wood-burning cooking stove, two bedsteads and two little cupboards in it. The other was empty except for a table and four chairs. When all our belongings were stacked in there, it looked dreadful. But Anneli was good at getting us organized. It was like playing at Mothers and Fathers: we made sofas from suitcases and wickerwork laundry baskets, with the upholstered seats from the barouche and cushions on top; bedside tables and sideboards from packing cases and wooden chests covered with curtains and headscarves according to size. Anneli, Vitya, Gerda and Fräulein Genzer sleep on mattresses on the floor. During the day, they cover their bedding with the old conservatory curtains. Anneli has made a sort of still life on her bedside box: photographs of boyfriends (**not** her so-called fiancé, Caspari!), poetry books and a bunch of flowers in a tooth mug. Nice.

I haven't got my own patch, as I share a bed with Mutti in the kitchen (or is it that we cook in the bedroom?) On the dining table we've spread the lovely linen tablecloth with the Bavarian peasant borders (folded double because the table is tiny) and on it stands a vase of roses. Roses from Mickelau which Väti brought. I'm willing them to last forever, but of course I know they will die.

VI. FOR JUTTA - 30 NOVEMBER 1944

Oh dear, how confusing life is: one moment everything is quite dramatically abnormal; the next, such ordinary things happen that it makes you wonder if anything has changed at all.

As soon as we were settled in Ebersbach (well, "settled" is an exaggeration; "accommodated" is a better word), Väti left us again, as instructed by the administrative authorities, to go back to Mickelau. So did nearly all the other men except the Mosins. As Russian refugees, they have most to fear from the Soviet army. Some of the Belgian prisoners-of-war stayed in Ebersbach, too, to look after our horses. Most of the men are urgently needed to help with the threshing in Mickelau, so that this year's exceptionally good harvest can be taken to safety in the Reich rather than fall into the hands of the Soviet army. Well...

They had trouble on the way: Günter (one of the farm apprentices) who was driving the rubber-tyred tractor, ran into a moving train on a level crossing. The tractor was a complete write-off. Günter was lucky enough to escape unhurt, suffering from nothing except a terrible shock. The authorities showed no sympathy about any of this. On the contrary, they got terribly worked up about the further delay in Väti's return, and when eventually he did report back, he was immediately arrested. He was allowed to send a message to Mutti by phone, asking her to come and see him in Trempen.

I didn't really understand what was happening. You know the infuriating habit grown-ups have of keeping unpleasant news from children. (Am I still a child? I'm confused even about that, in spite of my reluctance to grow into the silk-stocking age... if such things ever come into the picture again.) Off and on, words like "treason", "sabotage", "court-martial" slipped out in conversations between Mutti and Anneli, but if I asked what it meant, there was "nothing to worry about". You can imagine how that set me worrying! Cinema visions of executions at dawn; blindfolds being offered and refused by the brave; or whimpering cowards pleading for mercy, depending on whether they were the goodies or baddies... I couldn't see Väti fitting into either of these roles. But I was scared stiff.

I begged to be allowed to go with Mutti, and eventually she gave in – only, I think, because she didn't know what else to do with me. Anneli, like all the able-bodied people here, is called up to dig trenches round Ebersbach.

Then, confusingly, Väti rang again, to ask Mutti to bring – guess what! – his shotgun, for a hare shoot that he is hoping to organize in Mickelau. How on earth could I reconcile that with notions of court-martials?

The hare shoot – how I had always looked forward to that event! The date would be fixed well in advance, to avoid clashing with any of the neighbours' shoots, for every owner of a hunt round about was invited to everyone else's hunt. The men would arrive in the morning, clad in green loden jackets and matching hats with jays' feathers and goats' beards stuck in the band. They were brought to the farm by their coachmen, who would return late at night to pick up their masters: hare shoots were whole-day affairs.

36

In the autumn of 1943 I had for the first time been considered sensible enough to join the beaters. I was apprehensive about my involvement, as my sympathies were decidedly mixed. I didn't want the hares to die. They had too many pleasant associations: as Easter bunnies who hid nestfulls of eggs (previously dyed and painted by us – but I saw no contradiction in this); and as heroes of many of my favourite children's stories, especially the "Häschenschule"[8]. Nor did I want the beautiful foxes to be killed, even though I knew them to be ruthless and indiscriminate killers of our poultry, and had grown up singing the unsentimental

School for Hares

nursery rhyme, "*Fuchs du hast die Gans gestohlen*"[9]. On the other hand, I wanted our shoot to be a success, and success was measured by the number of corpses at the end of it. I would have loved Väti to become "King of the Hunt" – the one who had bagged the most game; but that never happened, to my knowledge. Unlike Onkel Arnold, Mutti's brother, who was huntsman first and farmer second, I think Väti only hunted because it was part of the farming process.

Shooting hares

And, of course, I was also excited by the adventure, especially as many of the Russian prisoners were among the beaters. It was ludicrous: there they were, strung out wide across the fields, with the guard vaguely behind them, his gun at the ready like the huntsmen but not, in his case, for shooting hares. We formed a more or less continuous human chain with which we would encircle a piece of ground.

"*Hoas op, Hoas op,*"[10] I shouted as loudly as the rest, anxious to impress Karp. But when the hare did as requested, and upped and dashed through our chain close to me, I squealed and ran after it. Luckily (or by design?) it was Väti who was behind me. "Get back!" he shouted, lowering his gun, "I could have got him!" "But he tried to escape!" I defended myself. "That's the idea, you fool, that's when we shoot them!" – And the Russians close-by, to witness my disgrace.

At midday, a box wagon came rumbling along the track from the farm. On it, a big milk churn full of piping hot pea soup with lots of Bockwurst sausages

---

[8] School for Hares
[9] "Fox, you took my goose away, give it back to me! Or else the huntsman gets his gun and shoots you, one two three!"
[10] "Jump up, hare"

swimming in it, and a large basket of thick slices of black rye bread. Hilde, the maid, ladled the soup into bowls for each of us, and we ate it, standing up around the cart. Never had our pea soup tasted that good!

I could have done without the afternoon session. My feet were soaking wet from trudging over muddy fields, and I was very tired. My sense of shame lingered. It had been made worse by a lecture from Väti over lunch about the dangers of accidentally getting shot. Nor was I cheered by the sight of a whole wagonload of dead hares and foxes preceding us to the farm, where they were displayed in front of a line of proud huntsmen for the customary photograph.

Mutti and Fräulein Genzer (Fräulein Genzer would have put it the other way round) had meanwhile prepared a grand dinner – mercifully not hare! After the soup course, Väti usually rose to his feet for the traditional toast to the "Weidmannskönig," the king of the hunt. "*Horrido!*[11]" he intoned, lifting his glass, and the whole gathering raised theirs and responded, "*Yoho!*" And again, "*Horrido!*" "*Yoho!*" And, even more loudly, a third time. I had grown up with this ceremony. But on one occasion, I don't know why, I got carried away and, instead of waiting to join in the response, yelled out at the top of my voice, "*Horrido!*" My childish voice rang out squeakily above my father's baritone. Everybody burst out laughing – except for Claus, who kicked me severely in the shins, and myself, who wished the ground would swallow me up.

I had been determined not to disgrace myself again in 1944. But could the shoot really go ahead, after we evacuated Mickelau?

On 7 November, Mutti and I set out, with me carrying that shotgun over my shoulder. Two of the Belgian prisoners (Lebrun and Fernand) came with us: they're to do a stint with the threshing party. We took a train to Insterburg. On the way, nearly everyone we met (not many: trains going east are almost empty) made some remark about me being the latest recruit to the People's Militia or, as one of them called it, the "hotchpotch" – old bones and tender young veg. Get it? Or is the People's Militia something purely for the defence of East Prussia, and you in your far-away new Saxon home haven't heard of it? It's like a sort of army composed of all the past rejects – all the men who are too old, too young or too unfit to join up. People say they will be armed with nothing but pitchforks. But that can't be true, can it?!

In Insterburg, we had lots of time before catching our connection with the narrow-gauge train to Trempen. So Mutti decided on a quick detour to your flat. As you know, I've still got my key to it. We sent Fernand and Lebrun ahead to the narrow-gauge railway station, and gave them the gun to look after. In case people got the wrong idea when they saw a prisoner with a weapon, we tried to camouflage it by wrapping bits of clothing round it. But you try and disguise a long thin thing like a gun! Fernand looked apprehensive, to say the least, but he's too much of a gentleman to refuse Mutti a favour.

---

[11] Hip hip – hurray!

Your flat... Well, of course, you know what it looked like: breakfast dishes all dirty on the table, a fried egg shrivelled on the kitchen stove. I bet that had been meant for you; I can almost hear the conversation between you and your mum: Come on, eat up, we don't know where our next meal will come from... I can't, I'll spew up... Mind your language...

Mutti tipped the egg neatly into the bin. Whatever for?! We nearly helped ourselves to some of the beautiful china that you had left abandoned in the sideboard, but what would have been the point of lugging it eastwards! All we did take was my printed writing paper: Marlene Wiemer, Mickelau, Angerapp District. Nothing but scrap paper now!

Breakfast how it had been at Mickelau

And just for that we missed our train. We had to take a bus for part of the way, and then cadged a lift on a lorry. The closer we came to Trempen, the more nervous I became: what exactly did it mean, Väti being under arrest? Would we find him behind prison bars?

Before I could find out, we were faced with another crisis: at the railway station in Trempen, Mutti was informed that Fernand had been picked up by a military patrol because of carrying that gun. The soldiers who kept him locked up at the railway station looked very grim and fearsome, and they took some convincing about the innocent hare shoot story.

By contrast, Väti's so-called prison was reassuring: a private house filled with civilians who wore armbands marked "People's Militia" (all old bones, no young veg., as far as I could see). Mutti and I were ushered into a tiny sitting room where we sat side by side on an old-fashioned plush sofa and waited and waited, while in the room across the corridor, the "trial" took place.

I discovered that Väti's offence wasn't just that he had been late returning to Mickelau after our evacuation: he was accused of deliberately planning that crash on the level crossing, so as to sabotage the rail link with the West. What an idiotic idea! As if Väti, of all people, would want to stop his crops being put to good use!

Every now and then, someone or other known to Mutti came to reassure her that he was on our side, but that the decision depended on the District Commissar, and he in turn had to act according to his instructions from I don't know whom, and so on.

In the beginning, my heart pounded in my throat whenever I heard the door at the other side of the corridor open. But as the negotiations went on and on and on, I felt nothing but boredom. We had to spend the night on that narrow sofa. I slept like a log, glad to know, at least overnight, what was expected of me. I don't know about Mutti, though.

In the morning, we were given the verdict: Väti was to be attached to the punishment battalion of the People's Militia in Ragauen. I was enormously relieved. But when Väti emerged, he looked ashen and old, and I wondered whether I had, in my usual way, got hold of the wrong end of the stick.

"It's good news, isn't it?" I asked him. "Except for the hare shoot..." (remembering about the shotgun).

"Mausie," he said, and hugged me tight, "The hares are the least of my troubles. If you saw the muddle in Mickelau nowadays... That's where I should be."

And it was only then, suddenly, that I understood what leaving Mickelau meant to him: Mickelau is his whole life. He wasn't bothered about us in Ebersbach, but he was bothered about the chaos in Mickelau. Now I'm icy with fear: how will he ever fit in anywhere else, away from Mickelau?

Well, we had to leave him like that, Mutti and me, and go back to Ebersbach. Mutti decided on the spur of the moment to make another detour and visit Omi Hahn in Alischken. She still calls that "going home", much to my annoyance: how can she be so disloyal to Mickelau? I know I'm unfair: I'll certainly go on calling Mickelau my home even when I'm married in some other place...

We didn't phone for a carriage to meet us at the station, but decided to walk to the farm, to give Omi a surprise. In this, we succeeded almost too well.

Omi Hahn's 80th Birthday, and in her Alischken garden 25 years earlier

I opened the kitchen door. There was Verushka, the Polish maid, cooking lunch. Omi, in her customary black widow's dress and apron, stood by the larder door, her big bunch of keys in her hand. A look of horror spread over her lovely crinkly face when she caught sight of us, and the keys clattered to the floor. I think she thought we were ghosts! But she soon recovered and, practical as ever, produced big jars of preserved meat and peas and carrots and morello cherries, and even the traditional biscuit tin full of meringues without which her household would be incomplete. Within minutes she had prepared a feast as for our family reunions in the past. And it **was** a sort of a family reunion: Tante Lena was there, and two of my cousins – Annelore and Ilse. Compared with Mickelau, nothing seemed to have changed here. And that, for some reason, struck me as more abnormal than the upheaval in your flat in Insterburg.

But in fact there were changes even here. For one thing, Tante Lena and family weren't visitors, they were refugees. They had left their own farm in Berschienen at the same time as we had left Mickelau, and had come to live with Omi. Onkel Arnold is one of those army officers who have recently been called up for training the People's Militia. Guess where: on his very own or, to be exact, Tante Lena's very own farm! I can't make out whether that's due to a clever bit of wangling or to a stroke of good luck.

My other two cousins – Usch and Kurt-Ulrich – weren't there; Usch because she has been called up to dig trenches somewhere or other. Kurt-Ulrich was evacuated to Saxony in the summer, with a school party. "Well, I just couldn't cope with him after Arnold had been called up," Tante Lena explained, "Always fooling around with air guns and ammunition, downright dangerous..." (Have I ever told you that he played at William Tell and actually shot an apple off Usch's head? I admire her for holding still even more than him for hitting the apple.)

What were their plans now, Mutti wanted to know. Tante Lena explained that Ilse would be sent to friends in Elbing, so that she could go to school. Mutti agreed emphatically: education was the most important thing in these uncertain times... My heart sank. She and Väti keep threatening to shunt me off to join you in Bautzen for the same reason...

As for the rest of them, they were waiting for the go-ahead from Onkel Arnold, and then Omi's and Tante Lena's combined trek would make for Pommerania, just the other side of the Polish Corridor. Omi's cousin owns a big farm there, with plenty of room for all, and why didn't we head there, too?

But Omi just sighed and said, surely it wouldn't come to that, and how could she possibly leave Alischken? She'd never done so since she got married, not for longer than a couple of days at a stretch (and then only under protest, as I knew from the many occasions when we had tried to persuade her to spend Christmas with us in Mickelau). Anyway, she said, even if the Russians did penetrate this far, it hadn't been so bad when they came last time, in the Great War, didn't Mutti remember?

I knew Mutti remembered: she had told me the story many times – how she used to rush out whenever there was a German cavalry unit riding along the main road, taking them baskets of fruit and biscuits (she was then the same age as I am now). One day, she was surprised to see unfamiliar uniforms. "Are you Austrians?" she'd asked as she handed out her apples. A flow of Russian had answered her. Then the Russians had searched the farm in case there were any German soldiers hidden away. One of the officers who spoke a little German had asked my grandfather whether, when this land became part of Russia after the war, he would take Russian nationality. "Yes, yes," my grandfather had replied. And Mutti's comment was, "I could have lynched him for that!" She's very

41

patriotic, is Mutti – which is funny when you consider how full of compassion she always is for all the foreign prisoners, and how she puts herself out to give them little treats... When the Russians had been beaten back that time, they had advised the people of Alischken in sign language to take shelter from the coming bombardment, so everyone had taken refuge in the gravel pit. And after a while, ventured out on to a little hillock to watch the Russian retreat: puffs of smoke from a line of separate explosions that moved steadily eastwards, and away from Alischken. Onkel Arnold, in his excitement, had swivelled a stick round and round so that it made a whooshing sound like a lot of horses at a gallop. "Cavalry!" someone shouted, and they all rushed for cover, including Onkel Arnold, who didn't realize that he was the cause of the misunderstanding. It's from this story that Claus and I got the idea for our games of "cavalry charge".

Maybe Omi is right, and it would be no worse being overrun by the Russians now, and all the tales of horror are just propaganda? Why should we be afraid of the likes of Karp and Vassili? I wish I knew.

You know those pictures they used to show us in biology, where you sometimes see black shapes on a white background, and at others white shapes on black? It happens to me with people's faces: they change suddenly into strangers, just by the way I look at them. For years I'd seen Omi as all granny-wrinkles and smiling blue eyes that went with walnut gateaux and parting presents of money. This time I discovered a new look on her face, strong and determined; the face not of a granny but of the owner of Alischken, farmer in her own right ever since my grandfather died long before I was born. And just as my new vision of Väti and Mickelau being one had made me shudder for him, I now worry about what will happen to Omi without Alischken.

You should be glad that Onkel Egon gave up farming years ago; I think townspeople are more moveable. Though whether that applies to you, who are part of Mickelau, I don't know.

VII. FOR JUTTA - 26 DECEMBER 1944

Can you believe it, we've come home for Christmas! From all the reports (official as well as unofficial) it seemed that Mickelau was still safe, at least for the time being. So Anneli and I pestered and begged Mutti to let us celebrate Christmas at home. At last she gave in, against her better judgement, I think. But when we discovered that Väti would get leave from the People's Militia to be there with us, she could hardly refuse. I must say, though, there have been moments when I thought we've been wrong to come.

Christmas time: what a jumble of memories that calls up in my mind – pictures and smells and sounds; and, above all, that tingling feeling of excitement, almost like pins and needles all through my inside… I had sleepless nights for the best part of December each year, starting on the night before the first Sunday in Advent.

That was when preparations for Christmas began. The kitchen was filled with a spicy scent that seemed to linger right through the Christmas season: cinnamon, cardamom, nutmeg, ginger… I used to think that that was the smell of frankincense and myrrh. A big lump of honey biscuit dough was pummelled and kneaded and then kept in the larder. Periodically, chunks of it were rolled out and cut into stars, comets, hearts, half-moons and gingerbread men, which were baked to provide an ever available stock of advent biscuits. Curly wrought-iron patterns of dough were left between the biscuit shapes. I used to eat them raw by the fistful.

On the Saturday before Advent, Frieda made the advent wreath. Whenever I helped her to cut the fir branches into even-sized twiglets, my fingers became tacky with resin and smelt of tangy forests. Frieda fixed the twigs with thin flower wire in a spiral round a central hoop of willow branch. Bright red ribbons, newly ironed, fastened the finished wreath to a bright red wooden stand, so that it swung clear of the table top like a miniature merry-go-round. Four candleholders mounted on pins were pushed into the wreath to hold four bright red candles. On special occasions, little chocolate fondant advent wreaths the size of curtain rings appeared as decorations on the wreath; put there, when I wasn't looking, by "Knecht Ruprecht", the servant of Father Christmas, no less.

That same character also managed to pop little gifts into children's slippers every night during advent, through a double thickness of glass! For at the onset of winter, Brodin, the wheelwright, put in an extra set of complete windows all round the house, to give us double glazing. Heavy felt window hangings with wool-embroidered canvas edges were then fastened to the lower part of the window frames, forming a sort of slanting roof over the sills. For years I used to think their main purpose was to provide a secret place for my slipper. I put it there between glass and curtain, and waited in suspense for the morning to reveal what I'd been given: an apple, some sweets, a handful of nuts? Or, as was known to befall naughty children, a stick? That happened only once to me, and I don't remember why, but I do remember clearly my horror when I found it there. I stood rooted to the spot, the cold seeping from the floorboards through my bare feet. Claus came to my rescue (experience had hardened him to such situations!). "You know what you do with that?" he said daringly, took the stick, broke it to pieces, and threw it into the waste paper basket. No wonder I love him.

But it was the **giving** of presents that weighed on my mind and gave me sleepless nights. It was taken for granted that I made all mine. I stitched together leather comb cases, embroidered book covers, glued pressed flower pictures, knitted ear muffs and knotted macramé bags with war time string made of twisted brown paper. All the work had to be done in secret. Which was why Mutti's presents were the hardest to make. For one thing, she was always about; for another, I often needed her help to get me out of calamities like dropped stitches and tangled threads. Once, I remember, I actually bought her a present. Omi took me to a big department store in Königsberg. She tactfully steered me past desirable china sausage dogs and gaudy flower vases as I had admired them in the Schalonkas' parlour. Eventually I chose a cut glass jam pot and had it gift-wrapped in elegant shop paper. For years I thought it the most beautiful object in the house. I don't know about Mutti...

Christmas Eve... The drawing room was out of bounds for me from the moment the fir tree was brought into the house, tall as the ceiling – too tall even for Väti to reach to the top without a chair. From then on, the doors remained firmly shut, opening only to allow Mutti, Anneli and the maids to scurry in and out. Occasionally, I caught a glimpse of silver sparkling through the crack, but I hardly needed the shouts of discouragement to make me look away: I almost felt as if the forbidden sight might strike me blind.

Skating

Anneli is better than her friend or Marlene Even standing still is an art

If the weather was right for skating, I joined the labourers' children on the pond, but on that occasion my heart wouldn't be in it. I would skate mechanically round and round, waiting for the signal that called me back to the house. I would change with lightning speed into my best frock.

And then the big double doors to the drawing room were flung open to reveal a brilliant glitter of candlelight on glass baubles and icicles of lametta. Sparklers showered stars of light onto the mountain of gifts under the tree. Which were mine? It was always a long time before I was allowed to find out.

Hilde, Marlene, Frieda, Jutta and Fräulein Genzer

First, we all sang carols. We were usually quite a big, resonant choir: our family, Fräulein Genzer, Frieda and Hilde, and also the three or four washer women who came to receive their annual gifts of a new apron and sweetmeats. We would lustily intone the old carol, "*O Tannenbaum, O Tannenbaum, wie treu sind deine Blätter!*[12]" In the days when the Father Christmas myth was still firmly kept alive, I could hear, in the silence between verses, the sound of sleigh bells coming closer. Then came the heavy knock on the door, and there was Father Christmas with his fur hat (just like Otto the coachman's best), white beard, and big serviceable sack (straight from the granary). His eyes were startlingly blue and kind, very like Otto's. But his voice was deep and growly and gruff when he asked me if I knew my Christmas poem by heart. This was the only horrible moment connected with Christmas. The skin on my cheeks would suddenly become too tight for me, as if it would burst from internal overheating. I would curtsey and rattle off my verses with as little expression as possible: to recite with feeling would have been soppy! The humiliation of getting stuck or, despite long practice, mispronouncing a word was increased by the knowledge that the grown-ups would smile indulgently and consider me "sweet". By the end of it, I always felt I had earned my presents.

I'm not conscious ever of a feeling of anti-climax after Christmas Eve. There were, after all, so many new games to play and books to read. Even visits to Omi, which usually took place on one of the holidays, were a bit of an unnecessary interruption. During the Christmas period, any day away from Mickelau was a loss. The whole of Christmas without Mickelau was unthinkable…

So home we went on the 24th. We went by train, a whole crowd of us: Mutti and me, Frieda, Hilde, and quite a few of the labourers' families whose men folk were there already for the threshing. Anneli was to follow later in the day, as she had

---

[12] "Oh Christmas tree, oh Christmas tree, how faithful is your foliage" – sung to the same tune as "The Red Flag"

to do her stint at trench digging first. Much to my annoyance, Mutti and I travelled Second Class, separate from the rest who, of course, went Third.

It had snowed a bit; but, instead of looking all Christmas-postcard-ish, it was more as though tattered sheets had been spread over the furniture when the painters move in, really dreary. All the farms we could see from the train looked ghostly, just the odd stray heifer nuzzling at stacks of straw. Even the roads were empty, except for a few army trucks. When I think of the congestion two months ago, when we moved from Mickelau...

Every so often, there were jagged red-brown gashes in the white. These were the famous trenches, I was told, like the ones Anneli is digging around Ebersbach. I must say, they're nothing like the trenches you see on the newsreels in the cinema. Heaven help Claus if he has to entrust his life to the protection of such seaside sandcastles!

Do you ever feel as though you'd been shoved into a corset and someone keeps lacing you up more and more tightly? That's what I felt like, going through that familiar landscape. Worst of all was the sight of a platoon of the People's Militia near one of the railway stations. There they were, shambling about in any old clothes, and a smart army officer yelling at them, "Left right, left right..." They tried, I think, to keep in step, but without any success whatsoever. Can you imagine Väti being drilled like that?

I felt like throwing myself across Mutti's lap and having a good cry. But there she was, all crumpled-up and old looking, and her eyes brimming with tears. Obviously, looking for comfort from mum is one of the luxuries of the past, like a bedroom of my own, and someone else to do the washing-up. Suddenly, we're supposed to be grown-up. Have you noticed the same change?

I couldn't bear it and went out onto the rattling little open platform at the back of the carriage, to get hypnotized by the wheels clattering over the rails beneath me. Remember the fun we used to have on these platforms on our weekend journeys from Insterburg to Mickelau? But sure enough, Mutti came rushing after me in her irritating way, to wrap a scarf round my face and tell me not to catch cold. As though I was, after all, just a little child!

Things cheered up a bit when we had to cadge a lift from the station in Trempen. There was a man with a tractor who is part of the Organisation Todt that are responsible for transporting grain from the abandoned farms to the West. By great good luck he was going exactly to Mickelau. So we clambered onto his trailer. Mutti looked glummer than ever. I wonder what she had expected: the usual coach and gleaming horses, with Otto sitting high and mighty on the box in his navy blue coachman's uniform? Well, Otto is in the army now, somewhere in the Polish Corridor (sorry, West Prussia, as they told us to call it at school). As for the horses, heaven knows what is happening to them at this moment: we left them scattered in their different stables in Ebersbach. Had you ever thought of horses as refugees?

I enjoyed bouncing about in the trailer, and I wished you'd been there with me. We would have sung at the tops of our voices when the birch trees of Mickelau came into sight, so familiar and beautiful, bare branches like filigree against the frost-blue sky. Mutti, of course, cried.

46

You won't find this so strange, being used to town life, but to me it was a new experience: when we got home, Mutti had to unlock the house. I don't think I had ever before seen the whole house locked and uninhabited.

And cold! Frieda set to and lit fires in the sitting room and dining room stoves and got the temperature rising fast enough. But it wasn't just that. Home? The place looked more like a furniture store. Chairs, tables and empty bedsteads were about all that was left.

Conservatory and back of house

I escaped into the garden as soon as possible. At least that was unchanged, except that the chrysanthemums had not been potted up and put in the conservatory for the winter but stood in the border, looking funereal. Someone had covered the rose beds with fir branches against the frost, as usual. It had never struck me before, but do you know what they reminded me of? Narrow elongated graves along either side of the gravel path.

View of rose beds and birch avenue from back of house

I kept chanting, "Mickelau, Mickelau..." to make me feel happy. But honestly, I wished we had never come back.

In the far corner of the vegetable garden some men were digging. Russian prisoners... I could have hugged them all, including ugly old Gregór. I shook hands with them, at least. But not with the guard! He looked more disapproving than ever.

When I went back into the house, there was a stranger in the kitchen. The face seemed familiar – Claus! He looked quite like a man, and I felt almost respectful towards him until he'd changed out of his uniform into his old breeches and sweater. And then Anneli arrived from the trench digging, and Väti from the People's Militia, and the house began to feel warm after all.

Claus fetched a beautiful Christmas tree from the woods. No need to take pity on the best and leave it for another year; what other year? It's funny not to have a future to think about. We decorated it with a few candle stumps and silver fir cones. No coloured balls: we'd packed those up when we left home. Imagine, refugees with a boxful of Christmas baubles!

The singing round the Christmas tree sounded a bit thin, and it got progressively thinner, until I could actually hear my own voice trilling forth! Of course, that made me stop at once. And so that left only Väti, loud and clear and, as usual, out of tune. I could have died with embarrassment. But nobody else seemed to notice. They were all too busy swallowing back their tears. Ah well...

I had quite a lot of presents, considering. But I can't be bothered to write about them. Somehow, they didn't seem to matter so much this year.

Tomorrow we're leaving again, almost as if of our own free will. There's hardly any noise from the front, just the odd bang to show it's still there. Which, in a way, is scarier than ever. It makes me feel like a mouse, with an invisible cat lying in wait, ready to pounce.

But I **am** glad we came home for Christmas.

VIII. FOR JUTTA - 1 JANUARY 1945

Happy New Year to you. As far as I am concerned, I must say I have my doubts about that, after such a wrong start: no party, no popping of champagne corks, no ringing-in of the New Year, and above all, no Mickelau... Even the family has shrunk to just Mutti, Vitya and me. Väti wasn't allowed to leave his Punishment Battalion; Claus, of course, is miles away, in the army training camp at Chemnitz, and Anneli has taken herself off for the night to a New Year's party at the front with Caspari and that lot. Gerda is no longer with us: just before Christmas she went back to her parents, who have been evacuated to Pommerania. We're still stuck with Fräulein Genzer, but she, mercifully, retired early to curl up on her mattress, looking aggrieved.

Vitya went to sleep at his usual time. Mutti probably would have wanted to go to bed, too, but I was determined to see the New Year in, by hook or by crook! So Mutti made a valiant effort to create a festive atmosphere by brewing up a sort of punch bowl of redcurrant juice with what spices she could lay hands on. We sipped this from our plastic mugs, which we clinked together every so often to say "Prost". "Clink" is quite the wrong word; "thud" would be more descriptive of the noise we produced. It wasn't at all like the romantic tinkle of glass. Hilarious!

We played quarrel patience; an exciting game, as you know. But in spite of that, the time until midnight really dragged, and I could hardly keep my eyes open.

That could never have happened in Mickelau. For as long as I can remember, I had been allowed to see the New Year in. There had always been a mad party, with a house full of visitors, and dancing and drinking, and jokes and games. Even the grown-ups behaved childishly. They tipped confetti over one another's heads, and tied up dancing couples in twisty snakes of paper streamers, and Mutti embarrassed me with her flirtatious giggles.

We went through all sorts of ritual to predict the future. We melted little lumps of lead in old metal spoons held over the flame of a candle. Sometimes they were specially bought lucky charms, and sometimes just the crumpled-up metal caps off wine bottles. When they became liquid, we tipped them into a bowl of cold water where they hardened into bizarre shapes from which we tried to tell each other's fortunes. In that same bowl of water, we floated lumps of charcoal, one to represent ourselves, and another for our boyfriend. If the two lumps collided and clung together in the whirlpool created by stirring up the water, there would be a wedding that year; if they met and parted, the course of true love would not run smoothly; and if they were flung apart in ever widening circles, it was best to give up the affair at once. As I couldn't make up my mind as to who my boyfriend was, I cheated by changing names halfway, and then disqualified myself for cheating.

Sometimes a troupe of bizarre gate-crashers pushed their way into our already crowded drawing room: the hoodeners. They were greeted with great joy, and were supposed to be good fun. I failed to see it that way. The tall stork snapped his metre-long beak viciously at me; the white horse lolled its ugly head from side

49

to side and threatened to stamp on my toes with its shambling, badly co-ordinated legs. All of the weird creatures stared at me from ghostly eye-less sockets. I was always glad when they moved on to the kitchen at the promise of food and drink.

At the stroke of midnight, we clinked our glasses together and hugged and kissed and said, "Prost Neujahr!" to cheer in the New Year. And then we children rushed out to ring the big farmyard bell over the bull shed. It sounded deafening in the frosty midnight silence, much louder than ever it did when Heiland, the foreman, rang in the start of work. And then we made a tour of the labourers' cottages to wish them "Prost Niejoar!" in the East Prussian dialect. Only after that was I content to go to bed, confident that the future would be as good as the past.

But this time? The beginning of 1945 looked bleak to me.

*There's nothing I look forward to on this New Year's Eve, I only look back. Isn't that what **old** people do?*

It is all settled that I'll come to live with you in Bautzen. Mutti will escort me there by train, leaving Anneli in charge of the trek in Ebersbach. I'm still arguing like mad to make them change their minds, but without much hope of success. Sorry! After all those weeks when I've been longing for your company... I now realize that I've always thought of it only in terms of you being with us, not the other way round.

"Towns are not for me" – panorama of Bautzen

It isn't that I enjoy living in this dump: it is deadly boring. Nothing to do, nothing to read, nowhere to go. At first, I used to spend a lot of time going round all the houses where our labourers' families had rooms. But now, most of them have been evacuated by train to different places west of the Vistula, except for the men (including the Belgians and White Russians) who are still in Mickelau to work for the threshing squad. That leaves only Opa and Volodya Mosin (Vitya counts as one of our family, now more than ever); and with them, the language problem becomes too exhausting after a bit. Hanging around by the horses isn't much good either, as they're so dispersed in other people's stables.

50

So why on earth don't I jump at the chance of being with you, the one person I know I can talk to and be understood? Maybe I'm just cussed like Fräulein Genzer? When Mutti told her that she should leave on the next special evacuation train, she sobbed, "If you threaten to send me away, I'll cough and cough all night so that none of you can sleep, then you won't ever be able to forget what you've done to me!"

You can imagine how she gets on my nerves! Just to look at her irritates me: her frizzy greyish hair growing like mould round her shrivelled-lemon face that always seems on the verge of tears. Even in Mickelau she never used to be exactly cheerful company. Since we've left home, she behaves as if we were her worst enemies, and you'd have thought she would have wanted to get away from us as soon as possible. But no amount of Mutti's reasoning would convince her that it was for her own good to be evacuated. I think she only wants to stay in order to spite us. Mutti says it's because we're the nearest to a family she's got. She's lived with us ever since I can remember. If Mutti hadn't reminded me, I would have forgotten all about her one attempt to break away from us:

Apparently, Fräulein Genzer had put an advert in the newspaper years ago, to find herself a husband. She had lots of replies – perhaps because she had included in the particulars of her attractions, "small savings account". Eventually she went to live with one of her applicants as his housekeeper. Mutti, with foresight, had kept her job in Mickelau open. And sure enough, she was back with us within months, heart-broken and disillusioned, and glad to be back, in spite of the fact that people on the farm made fun of her and her failed romance.

Maybe I should try my hand at blackmail like Fräulein Genzer? How about, "If you threaten to send me to Bautzen, I'll fart and fart all night so that you'll never forget..."?

But it's no laughing matter. It's very definitely a crying matter – only I'm not even allowed to cry. When I last saw Väti, and he kept going on about my need to go to school to get qualifications to earn a decent living blah blah blah, I burst into tears in front of everyone, and then he got really angry – angrier than he's ever been with me in all my life. You know how he's always spoilt me, and how, because of that, the others always sent me to him with any risky requests or confessions on their behalf! Well, this time he yelled at me as if I were Claus: couldn't I see how hard all this was for Mutti, without me making it worse, et cetera, et cetera.

"Hard for Mutti", I like that! And what about me? She only needs to change her mind, but I'm being shunted off willy-nilly, like a piece of furniture that they want to preserve for "after the war", and I can't do a thing about it. The worst of it is that there's only one place where I can hide myself away from all the rest, and that is the famous two-seater. And it's so very, very cold out there nowadays...

On the train   10 January 1945

And here I am, rattling through the night on a train jam-packed with refugees and all their paraphernalia. We, too, have oodles of luggage, because Mutti is yet again hedging her bets and dispersing her possessions. Being nicely brought up, as you know, I wanted to give up my seat to an old man. But – wonder of wonders – Mutti said not to bother! Well, I didn't have to be told twice. Now I sit with my nose glued to the window so as not to draw anybody's attention. I've found a peephole in the blackout shutter through which I can look out onto a dark grey world.

The train is taking me closer and closer to you, but it feels as if the opposite is true. I know I have changed since I left Mickelau, and I bet you have, too – so will we still get on together? If only I could imagine what this Bautzen is like! Only one letter from you has reached me, and that was written so soon after you got there that it tells me nothing except that "the surroundings are beautiful".

Leaving Ebersbach wasn't at all difficult. I felt a bit like crying when Opa Mosin and Volodya said good-bye to me, but I had to concentrate so hard on understanding Opa's good wishes in Russian that it distracted me. Although we've lived with our landlords, the Podlechs, for over two months, they don't mean a thing to me. I had to be reminded to say good-bye to them too. Anneli came as far as Königsberg to see Mutti and me onto our train. She was so matter-of-fact that you couldn't think of tears.

Going over the Vistula was like a film: the black outline of the bridge against the night sky, and here and there a soldier with steel helmet clamped on his head and gun at the ready keeping guard. And deep below us, the glittering water of the river that separates East Prussia from the Reich. That's when I cried. How stupid, to be reduced to tears by a river! But somehow "the other side of the Vistula" was like another name for Exile.

IX. BAUTZEN - WINTER 1945

The months that followed were the most – the only? – truly unhappy time in my life. It seemed to last for years, and I still feel that the calendar is cheating when I check the dates and discover that they add up to no more than eighty days.

Here I was, living in a town, an unfamiliar town at that, with no weekend visits to Mickelau to help me through each successive week. Suddenly I was cut off from my family and all my childhood friends, and each day felt more convinced that I would not see any of them again.

I was desperately homesick. I had grown such long roots in the fertile soil of Mickelau during the first thirteen years of my life! Perhaps that, in the end, made me able to withstand the transplanting all the better. But in the winter and spring of 1945, I was like a grubbed-up bush dumped by the roadside, roots tangled and stretching uselessly into emptiness.

The small adjustments in my life were bad enough. For example, I had never before bought any of my clothes by myself. Now, faced with an allocation of clothing coupons, I felt paralysed: how could I decide whether I needed a blouse or a skirt, whether these pyjamas were better value than those? In the end, I played safe and bought exactly the same garments as Jutta, even down to my pants.

At home, there had been two seamstresses who came to stay periodically to do all the family sewing. Fräulein Zeising specialized in shirts for Väti (two sets of detachable collars and cuffs for each), and in the household linen. Pillow cases and quilt covers, some of them in hand-loomed linen, were embellished with tiny tucks and insets of lace and neatly embroidered monograms so florid that they were like a puzzle to decipher. Fräulein Zeising was, as far as I was concerned, pretty and gentle and harmless.

My troubles began when Frau Kerutt took up residence. She mumbled through her big teeth, lips bristling with pins, and she tormented me with prolonged trying-on sessions. She made me twist and pirouette in front of her, and lift my arms just so high – like a submissive chicken lifting its wings when about to be caught. She pinned the new garment around me, and then eased it off, with little regard for the scratches she inflicted on me in the process. Nor did I consider the finished dresses as compensation for my pains. I hated new clothes, and would happily have spent all my days in Lederhosen or track suit, according to season.

The only aspect of Frau Kerutt's visits that I enjoyed was going through the waste bin at the end of each day, to retrieve interesting scraps of material in lovely shapes and textures. I hoarded the best pieces in the hope of turning them into Christmas presents, but usually underestimated the amount that was needed – allowing for seams – even to make little pin cushions. Or I tried to stitch them together into skirts and blouses for my dolls, but never allowed for enough space to get the clumsy creatures in and out of these clothes.

In any case, the period of mothering dolls was short-lived. Jutta and I used dolls as puppets rather than as babies. We dragged them round the farm, acting out impromptu plays through them. Our favourite character was an aristocratic lady whom we named "Frei-Fräulein von Frau". She spoke in the stilted language

53

that we associated with visitors from the "Reich"; she found farm life coarse and vulgar, and – of all the despicable, sissy things! – complained when she got her elegant outfits dirty. We ourselves, of course, never minded being caked in mud: we had nothing to do with washing our clothes.

Wash days in Mickelau were fun. Three washerwomen, wives of the farm labourers, came to the house once a week and filled the kitchen, not only with soap suds and steam, but also with singing and laughter, and jokes that I didn't understand. I would have loved to join in and help, but it wasn't considered safe for children to come anywhere near the boiling coppers. My only contribution to wash days was handing up the pegs when the clothes were being hung out in the garden. A clothes line was rigged up between the birch trees on the lower lawn. It criss-crossed the lawn like an intricate system of telegraph wires: we needed hanging space for at least eight sheets, feather bed covers, pillow cases, towels, a large number of tea towels and aprons, as well as the family clothes.

It was fun, too, when the clothes were dry and had to be folded. Two people gripped the corners of the sheets and pulled the material diagonally. Then they lifted their arms as high as possible and brought them down with full force, so that the sheet slapped like a sail caught in a wind. When I was very small, I used to crouch underneath and wait for the sudden whoosh of air above me. Then the sheet was folded twice lengthways, with another diagonal pull if necessary. And then the two women advanced on each other, for one to take both ends, and the other to catch hold of the fold in the middle. This, too, was repeated before the folded sheet was placed in the basket ready to go to the mangle. The whole performance had the formality of a carefully choreographed minuet.

But wash days in Bautzen, oh dear. Here, Jutta and I were often responsible for all the Kowalewski family wash. The clothes would be soaked the night before in a tub in a dank cellar room reserved for this purpose. The following morning, we had to roll up our sleeves and plunge our hands into the cold grey slime in order to fish out various garments as though from a Lucky Dip. Much the worst objects were Grandmother Kowalewski's long black woollen stockings. We were supposed to push our hands right down into the toe and turn them inside out. For some reason, my stomach always heaved as though it were treated in the same way.

Ironing was another job that had been taboo for me in Mickelau. Clothes were sorted into two categories: those to go through the mangle, and those for ironing by hand. It took two women to carry the laundry to the mangle, in the kind of two-handled wickerwork basket that doubled as Moses basket when there was a baby in the house. The mangle stood in the wheelwright's joinery. It was a rectangular table on which stood a large open box filled with stones. By pushing this box backwards and forwards, you activated a set of rollers at the bottom, through which the sheets were fed. It was too heavy even for the maids and was mostly operated by two men. I remember years of unsuccessful attempts at making the box move with my own strength. More often, I sat on top of the stones, to add my weight to theirs.

The ironing was done in the all-purpose room next to the kitchen. Frieda would pick out pieces of glowing charcoal from the kitchen range to put into the charcoal iron. She would test the heat of the iron by touching the base with a finger that she had previously spat on – a very daring feat that I longed to copy. To increase the heat, she would swing the iron back and forth with outstretched arm. You could see the red glow through the air holes, and sometimes a shower of sparks would fly through the room. There was the occasional scorch mark, or a smudge of ash that had to be dabbed off. If the finished article wasn't immaculate, it would relentlessly be returned to the laundry, especially my father's white shirts.

It seemed child's play, by comparison, to plug in the electric iron in Bautzen. But when I used it, it was astonishing how many pleats and tucks appeared in clothes that were meant to be smooth.

However, I came to terms with the superficial changes in my life. What I could not cope with was the sudden lack of love. The Kowalewskis were so cold and undemonstrative compared with my own family. At home, mornings had started with hugs and kisses all round, and pointless but nonetheless precious enquiries on how we had slept (I always slept well!). Here, Onkel Egon set the tone for the rest of the day by making us say "Heil Hitler" with right arm darting upward in the Nazi salute, and sharp about it!

Onkel Egon's body was gnarled with rheumatism, and so, it seemed to me, was his mind. His cruel beaky nose stuck out the more because his narrow lips were usually tightly pinched. As an adult, I might have noticed that he was in pain, and felt sorry for him. As it was, I loathed him. Once, I unburdened myself in a letter to Claus. He sent me a sympathetic reply in outspoken army language: "It's beyond me to understand how people who once used to be country people like us can be so mean… You'll just have to grin and bear it and think (like I do whenever a sergeant bullies me), 'Lick my arse!'" The Kowalewskis found the letter, read it, and were brazen enough to confront me with their breach of my privacy. That killed off any dormant affection in me for them. Even for Jutta.

Once in the past, she had admitted that she felt more at home among us than with her own parents. Now, to my utter dismay, she aligned herself with them! When she had left Mickelau in October, she had written to me, "I don't know what's hit me: they complain if I burst out singing in the street, they criticize my muddy shoes…" Now she did the same things to me: she shushed me when I whistled, she tugged critically at the hemline of my coat in a vain attempt to cover my ever-lengthening legs (the clothing allowance didn't run to a new coat).

And worst of all, she seemed to prefer the actual presence of a pimply adolescent called Naser to the memory of Karp and Vassili. To me, that was a terrible betrayal of our sacred last summer in Mickelau, when we had been united in all we felt and thought. Would life go on like this forever? There seemed no way out.

Mutti had left me in Bautzen on 20 January, to go back to Anneli in our temporary home in Ebersbach. She had assured me that if the Russian offensive got underway again, she and our trek would make straight for Bautzen. She had already arranged with a farmer on the outskirts of the town to give accommodation to us all, including the horses.

But as I returned from seeing her off at the station, there was a telegram addressed to her from Anneli: "Am ordered to leave stop don't come." Too late. Four days later, a postcard and a letter from Mutti arrived, written in stages at various unscheduled stations to which she had been shunted on her attempt to go back to East Prussia. The last one came from Elbing, about 30 kilometres from Ebersbach. Then silence.

For the next three weeks my life seemed to consist of waiting for post and listening to radio news broadcasts, of crying myself to sleep and being woken by air-raid sirens. The Kowalewskis had a room with use of a kitchen in the Schliebenstrasse, but Grandma Kowalewski, Jutta and I slept in a little room across the road with a lady called Frau Rolle. She shared our dislike of the cellar cum air-raid shelter and didn't insist on us using it. The thought of getting trapped in that hole with its grey concrete walls, grey blankets and grey-skinned people, and its pervasive musty smell was our worst nightmare; but when the noise of passing planes and falling bombs came very close we did, illogically, dash headlong down the concrete stairs. Or when Jutta had romantic longings to join the dreadful Naser down there. Most of the time we stood on the back door step and watched the gruesome beautiful spectacle of star shells and fire-red skies over nearby Dresden, and listened to the whine and crash of dropping bombs that was so much more terrifying than the gunfire in Mickelau had been.

I was dutifully enrolled at school – ostensibly the main reason for my separation from Mutti. It was a Secondary Girls' School from Bremen that had been evacuated to Saxony to escape the British bombing raids over western Germany. It shared a building with the local school, each being allocated the classrooms for a few hours per day. But even during so-called lesson time, we were mostly given duty rotas in soup kitchens for refugee treks from Silesia. Their rack wagons looked stupidly out of place among the streets of the town and made my inside ache with longing for my own Mickelau trek.

News bulletins brought no consolation. We had laughed in the past about the much publicized way in which the British had presented their evacuation from Dunkirk as a victory. Now the German news reports excelled at their own versions of "victorious retreat": front lines were being "rationalized" as a better foundation for "final victory"; so and so many enemy troops were being obliterated in "decisive battles", without mention of the German losses or of the fact that the battles themselves had been lost. British and American bombers were shot down over an increasingly large number of towns, thus showing how widespread bombing raids had become.

I wasn't bothered about the German retreat in France or in southern Europe. To begin with, I didn't even take in the advance of the Red Army in Silesia, the front line nearest to Bautzen. To me, bulletins consisted wholly of reports on how one district after another in East Prussia and West Prussia (which I was still used to calling the "Polish Corridor") was "fighting heroically", though "temporarily cut off" by Russian troops.

Nor did the post bring me comfort. Instead of the longed-for mail from Väti, my own letters to him – a whole batch of them – were "returned to sender". Which, I decided on re-reading them, was just as well. My outbursts of homesickness and misery were not designed for cheering up a reluctant soldier in the front line. I cremated them ceremonially on the kitchen range when no one was looking.

Claus wrote twice, each time as anxious for news as I was; but at least that made me feel less alone. A letter from Caspari, written just before moving into the trenches, spoke of abortive attempts to meet Väti at his People's Militia punishment battalion, and of puzzlement over Anneli's recent coldness when he had contacted her in Ebersbach: "She seems more concerned for the health of the horses than for mine..." Poor Caspari. He sounded so unhappy that for a moment I almost forgot my own misery and was willing Anneli, over the distance, to be kind to him. But I knew from before I had parted with her that she had already regretted her romantic gesture on that last night in Mickelau when she had become engaged to him.

Jutta had made friends among the girls at the school in Bautzen. I was hardly aware of their existence, and when they were re-evacuated, back to their homes in Bremen (the British bomb threat now being considered as the lesser of two evils), they disappeared from my life without trace.

I was not allowed to ignore the Russian front near Bautzen for long. On 10 February, the town was declared a "fortress"; a strange phrase, with its medieval overtones, especially since Bautzen could actually boast of a fine old castle, perched high on a rock and surrounded with a moat and steep fortified walls. Had we gone back to medieval warfare?

What the phrase actually meant was that the town would be defended against the enemy "to the last man". And because of this, all civilians had to be moved out of the way. I desperately wanted to stay; not because I had developed any ties to the place but because I did not want to be cut off from my Bautzen address – my only immediate point of contact with my family.

My body came to my aid: I developed a dramatic attack of tonsillitis. Being ill was nothing new to me. I had often had sore throats in winter, even after my tonsils had been capped which was supposed to have cured me. What was new was to be ill without Mutti.

Mutti made a fuss over any illness. Although this irritated me when I didn't feel too bad, it was lovely when I felt rotten. She had several remedies for different symptoms: for coughs, hot milk and honey. The fact that it was well known that Mutti herself hated this drink enhanced its medicinal reputation. For sore throats, our necks were wrapped first in one of Väti's large white handkerchiefs dipped in water, and then several layers of silk and wool scarves. 'flu or any other illness involving a high temperature was cured with a sweat bath. For this, I usually moved into Mutti's bed. I was given an aspirin and a drink of piping hot home-made redcurrant juice. Then I was smothered to the tip of my nose in feather beds and told not to move for the next twenty minutes or so, in case I sprang a leak in my cocoon. To pass the time, Mutti would read to me – all the traditional fairy tales over and over again. On the whole, I preferred Hauff's to the Grimms', although the latter left a deeper impression: it was our heavy feather beds from the spare room that I saw Mother Holle shake from the skies to make snow; the golden ducats of the "Sterntaler" were the golden birch leaves that I tried to catch as they fluttered on to our drive in the autumn; the magic table of "Tischlein deck dich"[13] had been made in our wheelwright's joinery; and, most haunting of all, the severed head of Fallada the horse that was impaled on the gloomy archway and talked down on the wronged princess in the "Goosegirl" belonged to one of my favourite mares.

As I became older, Mutti added the sad tales about bears and foxes by Thompson-Seton, and the even sadder stories of "Sayo and her Beaver Folk" and "Little Brother" by Grey Owl to the repertoire. There was also an uplifting moral tale in a fat dilapidated volume of which I remember nothing but a chapter heading: *"Not lehrt beten"* [14], and the fact that the heroine, living through extremes of misery and despair, dropped on her knees and prayed to God and, hey presto, her troubles were over.

This phrase, *"Not lehrt beten"*, came back to me again and again as I lay on my lonely sick bed in Bautzen. I decided to give it a try: Please God let Mutti come; please God let me go back to Mickelau. It didn't work even as a comforter. Jutta and I had, in many soul-searching discussions, argued God out of existence, and I was aware that my prayers were no more than the superstitious formula that I enacted at first sight of a New moon: curtsey and wish, and your wish will be granted. I didn't believe in that either, but it couldn't hurt to keep trying.

The only thing that gave me a sort of comfort was my complete abandonment to self-pity: I crawled under my feather bed and cried and cried. Poor Tante Louise, she must have been nearly out of her mind with worry; but I never gave a thought to that.

Because of my illness, we were allowed to delay our departure from Bautzen for a week. Long enough for the letter from Mutti to reach me. We were packed up and ready to leave by the next refugee train to Schwarzenberg in the Erz mountains when the postman arrived.

The letter was oddly reassuring, even though it had been written a fortnight earlier and came from an area which, according to the latest news bulletins, had long since fallen to the Russians. "We are near Danzig," Mutti wrote, "Completely stuck in blizzards and overcrowded roads. We'll abandon the trek and everything and go on by train as soon as we can get one; but they say there aren't any…"

But the best part of the letter was a postscript… from Anneli! All she said was, "Wish you were here – but really I'm glad you're safe in Bautzen."

At last a sign that Mutti and Anneli had found each other! At last I knew that they were together, instead of blundering about separately in the snow, as I had seen them nightly in my imagination! I felt cured of my illness almost instantly.

But it was many weeks later that I heard the full story of how they had come to be reunited.

Three days after leaving me, Mutti had come to a dead stop in a place called Mühlhausen. She was told that all train services going east had been cancelled,

---

[13] Table lay thyself
[14] Distress teaches us to pray

and that all those areas – including Ebersbach – had already been evacuated. But as she didn't know what else to do, she decided to walk to Ebersbach, all the same. So there she had been, on a road crowded with refugee treks, the only person going resolutely in the wrong direction.

"Just look at that," Volodya had said to Anneli, pointing at the dark shape that trudged towards them through the drifting snow. "It's sure to be a woman. When women get confused, they go looking for what they've lost; men run away."

Mutti had recognized the horses before she could identify the mummified shape on the coachman's box of the barouche. "Well, here I am, at last," she'd said cheerfully. "Thank God I met you."

Anneli's reaction had been more complicated. Pleasure, of course, but also shock and irritation: how could Mutti have risked the return journey!

The evacuation order had come to Ebersbach that morning, on 23 January. Anneli, together with all the other refugees in the village, had been told to leave with just as much luggage as they could carry: army lorries would transport them to the nearest railway station to continue their journey west by train. The roads were too congested to take more horse-drawn treks. From the start, Anneli had been tempted to defy this order. To leave the horses behind? They were so much more than livestock, they were personal friends!

When it turned out that only German nationals were allowed onto the lorries, the decision had been easy. Of course she had to stay together with Vitya, Volodya and Opa. So they had hurriedly set out: Opa Mosin on their panje-cart drawn by the faithful old pony from the Russian steppe; Volodya on a rack wagon drawn by four horses, with two spare horses tied to the back, and a month-old foal roaming loose; "Big Vladimir", a young deserter from the Soviet army who, with his wife and baby had been with us since the autumn, nervously mounted on Illyrier, our temperamental stallion; and Anneli on the coachman's block of the barouche, with Vitya and Big Vladimir's family as passengers. They had taken a side track to avoid the worst congestion of the main road. So it was by pure chance that they had come upon Mutti.

"Let's go back to Ebersbach," Mutti had suggested innocently, "Now that I've come this far, I'd like to say good-bye to the Podlechs and thank them for their kindness…"

Anneli, exasperated beyond words, had ignored her and angrily whipped the horses into a canter. Soon after that, they had seen the first Soviet tank roar past on the main road to Elbing.

X. SCHWARZENBERG - SPRING 1945

Schwarzenberg in the Erz mountains was an odd place to come to: the little town seemed completely cut off from the rest of the world by a wall of mountains that closed in on the houses from all sides and almost shut out the sky. I had the feeling that it should be inhabited by gnomes hammering away at legendary swords, not by human beings – least of all by refugees from the wide open plains of East Prussia. Even the forest of tall red brick factory chimneys had a fairy tale quality for me, as I had never seen anything like it.

The journey had been horrible. We left Bautzen in the dark, and we arrived in Schwarzenberg in the dark, having taken almost twenty hours to cover a distance which would, under normal circumstances, have taken less than two. Each of us wore several sets of clothes to cut down on the luggage we had to carry. A theory that failed to take into account the difficulty of carrying anything in arms as stiff as though encased in plaster.

For the third time in five months I had to rethink which of my private treasures I valued most. The "war heroes" had been left behind in Mickelau; the exercise books with the dog kennel designs ended up on the Ebersbach rubbish dump. Now I wrenched myself away from my "art collection" – reproduction postcards of sculptures in the Nazi-approved heroic style. Anneli had told me long ago that they were "kitsch", and I had begun to suspect she was right. I also abandoned a china dog that was a substitute for my beloved "Maya", the dachshund I had left in Anneli's care in Ebersbach.

I hesitated a long time about my lucky horseshoe which had been dropped, months ago, by one of the Mickelau horses. Eventually, I compromised by prising out one of its nails and a few crumbs of Mickelau mud, which I wrapped in a scrap of notepaper and kept in my purse for many years. "Essential luggage" included my diary, my photo album, and a framed picture of Mickelau. I was determined to hang onto them, come what may. I also felt obsessively responsible for the bulky bundles of heavy linen table cloths and napkins which Mutti had entrusted to me.

Our train had been scheduled to leave Bautzen at four in the morning. When it eventually pulled into the station at six, it was already overcrowded with refugees from Silesia and their possessions. After some shuffling around, our party managed to find seats, split up over several compartments, only to be told in the outskirts of Dresden that we would be transferred to buses in order to cross to the other side of the city. The railway was out of action.

Dresden. Before I had left East Prussia, I had been told again and again what a beautiful town Dresden was, and how lucky I was to have the chance of visiting it. Now I had got there, and all I saw was devastation: the result of those night air raids we had marvelled at from our cellar steps in the Schliebenstrasse in Bautzen.

We had heard rumours that in the night of 13 February, British bombers had "flattened" the city. It was the wrong word. A number of houses still stood upright in the vast field of rubble, roofless, split open lengthways, like a pig's carcass, spilling its entrails: doors, drain pipes, a dangling bath – signs that, once, life had been ordinary.

It never entered my head to worry about Onkel Rudi, the family friend into whose hands we had entrusted the Mickelau valuables on the assumption that Dresden was a safe place. I felt completely drained of any emotion. I concentrated wholly on my own comfort and my little pile of luggage.

When we changed trains at Chemnitz, I was vaguely aware that this was the place where Claus had gone for his military training, but I accepted without hesitation the fact that I could not break my journey to look for him.

But then our journey was broken, for all that, by the sound of air raid sirens, and we had to spend hours in the station shelter. Jutta's and my attention was caught by four youngsters of about our age but in full military uniform of some sort. They openly passed remarks on us in a language which they assumed was private to them, but which sounded sufficiently like Russian for us to understand. So we startled them by joining in the conversation. They told us they were Croatian cadets. Croatian? They explained as best they could in our limited common language that their home was in Yugoslavia, and no, they were not on the enemy side; it was the Serbs (who also lived in Yugoslavia) who were the enemy; in fact, the Hitler army were helping the Croats in their fight against the Serbs. Friends? Enemies? When the "all clear" siren sounded, the boys carried our luggage to the platform. "Do svidanya, do svidanya," we shouted after them. Only when Onkel Egon rebuked us sharply did we realize how tactless it was, among the throng of refugees, to bid them farewell in the "enemy" language, Russian.

When, at last, we arrived in Schwarzenberg, we were billeted in one of the many factories with the tall chimneys – a so-called "enamelling and metal stamping press". When we asked what exactly that meant, we received evasive answers which led us to assume that it had something to do with the manufacture of arms. Day and night, our ears were assaulted by the buzzing of machines. I thought I would never be able to sleep again and would not have believed that before long it would be the sudden absences of sound that would wake me, even before I heard the air raid sirens.

Our "home" for the next three weeks consisted of five beds in a dormitory of twenty-three, which were occupied by as many adults, plus a fair number of children who shared beds with their parents. On each bed lay a mattress of sacking stuffed with straw – or so we thought, and marvelled that even the local straw should be inferior to the comfortable East Prussian kind. Later, we discovered that it was really a particularly hard kind of wood shavings. Of course! There was hardly a farm worthy of the name for miles around.

Jutta and I spent our time observing our fellow inmates. We made ground plans of the dormitory, rather like the dog kennels designs we had just jettisoned in Bautzen, and labelled each bed with a nickname we thought appropriate to its occupier. We were astonished by how differently people reacted to the same circumstances.

On the one extreme were the "Misery-A's" and the "Misery-B's". Their conversation consisted of exchanging moans and groans among themselves, and finding fault with the rest of us. Hardly a day passed when one of them didn't pick a quarrel with the factory authorities. Mr Misery-B was confined to bed with a ghastly cough which he used to dramatic effect. He would burst into a stream of abuse, shouting and raving until he was convulsed with a fit of coughing. He then turned crimson, gasped for breath, stretched his arms heavenwards and, with an accusing look at the object of his wrath, sank back on his pillow. Cheerfulness was his worst irritant, which was why a group of orphans and their "aunties" from a children's home in Königsberg most frequently fell foul of him.

But even he couldn't squash their good spirits. They cheered our official waking-up times with a dawn chorus, and sang us to sleep with gentle East Prussian and Silesian folk songs. Soon they received orders for special birthday serenades, which they performed with a real sense of occasion around the bed of the "birthday child", clutching the burning stump of their emergency candle and a little bunch of catkins, early greenery or stolen snowdrops. My birthday was among those celebrated in that way. Fourteen years old…

The girls looked after other people's children and supplied Jutta and me with reading matter. They also kept us informed on current affairs, for they had brought a radio with them – a remarkable feat in the days before portable transistors. It was one of the cumbersome *Volksempfänger*[15] that were sold cheaply so that the Ministry for Propaganda could spread its message among the masses. The Königsberg "aunties", however, tended to cut short the voice of Dr Goebbels, the Propaganda Minister.

We were fed communally in the factory canteen: an endless diet of watery soup made with dried swedes. On our first day, Tante Louise set us a good example by stoically ladling her way through her plateful – a wasted gesture, as she promptly sicked it all up again and so put us off the more thoroughly. But as there was no alternative, we soon learnt to swallow down our portions to stave off the worst of the hunger.

Hunger was now commonplace, especially when we moved from the factory to two rooms in a private house, and had to make do with our own meagre food rations. I watched Tante Louise with distrust and came to the conclusion, bitterly recorded in my diary, that it was Jutta who got the thicker slice of bread and the fuller ladle of soup. When the weighing scales revealed that I had lost 5 kg in weight during the three weeks since leaving Bautzen, as against Jutta's 2 kg, I thought Tante Louise's consternation was mere hypocrisy. Once, when I was sent to the baker's to buy bread, I nibbled off a little corner of the loaf. But only once: the accusations of selfishness that were heaped on my head made me burn with shame.

So much fuss about a bit of bread… In Mickelau it wouldn't even have been noticed. There, at least six loaves had lain side by side on the deal table beside the bread oven on baking days, heavy ovals, like giants' clogs, each about four pounds in weight, with cracked floury crusts. Half was made with wholemeal rye flour, the other half with refined rye flour; and sometimes, as a treat for those who liked it (but not for me) a white wheat flour loaf called 'Striezel'. The maids cursed over the kneading, up to their elbows in a trough-full of dough. The trough

---

[15] The People's Receiver

was scraped clean, but not washed, and a lump of dough was left in it until next time: the sourdough which acted as raising agent for the next baking day.

The bread oven was of the kind in which Hansel and Gretel disposed of the witch: a sort of cave of red brick, with a cast-iron door. A fire was lit inside this structure and left there until the correct heat was reached. The embers were then scraped out with a long-handled tool, the shape of a hoe, and the loaves that had been left to rise overnight were put in its place. The smell of freshly baked rye bread used to draw me to the kitchen from wherever I might be.

Spring came to Schwarzenberg, and the mossy smell of melting snow almost overpowered that of sooty factory smoke. I had no intention of becoming optimistic, and I had little enough cause; but somehow the weather brought it about automatically.

Schwarzenberg

I wanted to go for walks in the mountains. But Jutta, for some reason, was nearly always "too lazy..." "too tired..." "not in the mood..." She irritated me enormously, the more so since I felt too dependent on the Kowalewskis' good will to pick a quarrel.

Sometimes I ventured out on my own. Outside the town, the countryside was beautiful: dark forests of low-hanging silver fir trees clung to such steep slopes that it made me wonder how they could keep their hold; streams and little runnels of melted snow flowed towards the valley at a speed which amazed a plains child like me. No hope of following a stick-boat downstream: it either disappeared from sight or got flung against the rocky banks.

There were no big farms here, just small homesteads surrounded by pocket-handkerchief-sized fields. Peeping through the door of an outbuilding, I saw a brown cow – an exotic sight that I knew only from picture books and the wrappings on milk chocolate. I was only used to black and white Friesians! The chickens, too, were of an unfamiliar breed, funny white speckled things.

Seen from the distance of a mountain side, the factory chimneys of Schwarzenberg looked like tall tree trunks with their tops blown off. It was all very interesting and strange – and slightly scary.

Only the spring smells were the same as in Mickelau: dank earth, new out of its winter wrapping of snow; tangy fat buds bursting into greenery that smelt like Frieda's skin cream. They increased my homesickness, but the sensation itself had begun to change: beside the eye-stinging pain of it, there was now also the joy of remembering... All that beauty, all that happiness I had known in Mickelau.

At home, we used to have expeditions to the woods in early spring – Mutti and I, Claus, Anneli and any number of cousins or friends who happened to be about. We took little baskets with us, in case the wild hepatica were in flower. The sky-blue carpet of blossom proved irresistible to our greed: we picked so many that we grew tired of arranging them later in little bowls and shallow moss gardens, and Frieda was fed up with having to dust round them on every table top and sideboard.

In the woods, we children used to pick up stout sticks that served as theatrical props for many roles. When I was younger, I straddled mine to gallop ahead of the main party on my fiery steed. Or we were mountaineers, even though the only "mountains" were the banks of ditches. Or we were jungle explorers, hacking our way through thickets and fending off ferocious animals. Whenever we heard a crackling in the undergrowth, we'd frighten each other with talk of wild boars. These were a real possibility: bears and wolves, which visitors from the "Reich" expected to find in the wilds of East Prussia, were not. There was a story about the trick my uncle Gustav played on his visitors from Berlin: the young couple had recently become engaged and went courting in the woods. Onkel Gustav followed them, dressed up in a bear skin which he had brought back from his adventurous past in Canada. When the young couple saw this so-called bear come crashing through the trees, the man took to his heels, with never a backward glance at his fiancée. As a result – so the story goes – the wedding was called off.

Just as the hepatica in the woods were a sign that spring had arrived, so were the baby chicks on the farm. There had always been several families of chicks in Mickelau: pale fawn Rhode Island Reds with their chestnut coloured mother hens, or the yellow baby chicks of the white Leghorns, or even, like cuckoos in the nest, a clutch of speckled guinea fowl with a Leghorn broody hen to look after them. I never cared much for these happy family set-ups, with their possessive mother hens trying to keep me away from their babies. As far as I was concerned, there was a lot to be said for the day-old-chicks that Mutti bought each year.

It was a tense moment when she walked into the kitchen carrying a large flat cardboard box that had penny-sized air holes punched into it at intervals. Excited chirps emanated from the box, and when I put my hand underneath it, I felt a constant tingle of movement, almost like pins-and-needles. Then the lid was taken off to reveal a collection of Easter decorations: fluffy lemon-yellow balls packed tightly together, softer to touch even than a horse's nostrils.

In a corner of the room between kitchen and dining room, a little enclosure of wire mesh had been rigged up, in the centre of which stood a kind of substitute mother: a paraffin heater with a spreading metal hood under whose warmth the chicks sheltered as under the outspread wings of a broody hen. For the next few weeks, the characteristic smell of this room was a mixture of damp oat flakes and feathers.

Gradually the chicks went through a process that was the reverse of the Ugly Duckling story: as the white top feathers began to sprout between the yellow down, they lost their cuddly beauty and became rather plain. By that time they were ready to be banished to colder quarters: a mobile chicken hutch in the farm yard. This was a waist-high structure similar to the one in which Claus kept his angora rabbits, but instead of wire mesh doors, there was just a tiny flap that slid open to allow the chicks to run in and out. If people wanted to get at the chicks, they had to prop up the hinged roof of the hutch like the lid of a chest, and stick their heads in from the top.

Again and again I was warned not to knock against the strut that kept the lid open. That warning had a fatal attraction. "You must not touch it" was like a challenge to get as close as possible without touching it. So it wasn't really surprising that one day the calamity happened: while Anneli was bent double, deep into the chicken hutch, the lid came crashing down on top of her.

The old garden veranda, before it changed to a conservatory...

Just enough space to hide after knocking your sister's head off

I didn't wait to see her headless torso drop to the ground; I didn't wait to see the severed head rolling obscenely among the startled chickens: I ran. My legs carried me straight to the garden side of the house. The garden veranda was raised on stilts of brick, just high enough for me to fit under. I shot down there, like a rabbit running for cover. And I cowered behind the furthest pillar. During games of "hide-and-seek", this was an almost fool-proof hiding place. On those occasions, it held no threat for me: while I sat there, ready to dash for "home"

65

when I had seen the feet of the "he" move past, the smell of dank mouldering leaves reminded me of lovely autumn days. But on this occasion, it smelt of witchcraft and death, and the darkness was crowded with evil creatures from my Illustrated Grimms' Fairy Tales. And there was no "home" in the terms of the game – no safe refuge – to run to. I watched lots of feet walk past: Frieda's and Hilde's wooden clogs, Mutti's flat-heeled walking shoes, Anneli's pretty sandals – yes, Anneli's! But I was too far gone in my terror to realize that that meant Anneli was alive. I heard all their voices enticing me back among the living; but each time I just shrank deeper among the shadows. I died of hunger, of cold, of loneliness. The strip of sunlit ground outside my hiding place grew darker and darker. At last, I could bear it no longer, and when Mutti's tearful voice called me again, I crawled out. And home was "home" after all.

It was as if the thaw in Schwarzenberg brought about a spring awakening of the post: letters trickled in, re-addressed by the Bautzen post office which was still in action – from Mutti and Anneli, from Omi Hahn and Tante Lena, and from various relatives and friends who used me as a clearing house. All the world seemed to be on the move, nomads without an address of their own.

Mutti's letters, written at intervals over the last four or five weeks, arrived in an utterly erratic order of time with no relation to when or where they were posted. With regard to their contents, they were like unconnected pieces of a jigsaw puzzle, showing a bit of colour here, a snippet of pattern there. Would I ever receive the complete set, and would I be able to fit it together into a whole that made sense?

One of the recurring themes was a description of the various places where their little band had spent their nights: "We stayed with a miller's family, simple folk but very kind and clean..." "We were put up by the local baker, and even had a bed to share between the eight of us, an unexpected luxury..." "At the manor house of the Countess Schwerin we were able to have a good wash and even get undressed for sleeping. The owners themselves were just leaving and urged us to go, too; but our horses were at the end of their tether, as we'd travelled all the previous night and day." "The worst night for me was when we slept in a cowshed, because it was so cold, and I was so jittery for fear of mice; but it turned out all right and a good deal better than dozing on the wagons overnight in this fierce cold..."

Sometimes, Anneli's comments provided a different view: "Who would have thought that a sheep pen is the worst possible place to be cooped up in: the mixture of smells from their wool and urine is truly unbearable. Better by far to sleep among cows, except that you have to be alert when they lift their tails just above your head!!"

It was Anneli who told me the macabre tale of the deep-frozen granny. When people died, as happened with increasing frequency, they had to be left by the roadside: with temperatures around -30 °C, the ground was too hard for burial, and anyway, there was no time to spare. However, one particular family could not bear to part with their dead grandmother in such a callous way. They wrapped the corpse in a clean sheet and hung it from the back of their wagon, waiting for better times. The trouble was that many of the refugees also carried carcasses of

66

slaughtered pigs in this natural deep-freeze. And one morning, to the consternation of the bereaved, their granny had gone...

The main message that I received from these letters was that Mutti's trek, in spite of their slow progress and numerous hold-ups, had managed to outpace the advancing Soviet troops. Then, on 21 March, the first official day of spring, I received a postcard that gave me an address near Hamburg to which I could write poste restante. "It seems that after nearly seven weeks on the road we are approaching the end of our journey," Mutti wrote, "As soon as we are settled in, I shall come to Bautzen to fetch you."

To Bautzen! I wrote at once to tell her of my change of address, but with the delays in postal services, it was unlikely that my letter would reach her in time. Also, as the Russian and Western Allies moved towards each other, the unoccupied strip of Germany became narrower all the while. Judging by reports of other people's attempted journeys, it became increasingly improbable that Mutti would still manage to travel from her extreme north-western corner of Germany all the way to the Erz mountains near the Czechoslovak border.

Night after night, I dreamt about Mutti. I saw her very clearly, but sometimes we were in a crowded room and couldn't reach each other. At others, she looked at me blankly, without emotion, because she failed to recognize me. During day time, I was reluctant to go out, reluctant to do anything. I sat and watched the door. Nothing happened. Time dragged.

There had been two air raid warnings in the night of 4 April and, as a result, we slept long into the morning. There was, in any case, little point in getting up: there was nothing to do, and besides, one felt less hungry in bed. The doorbell woke us. Tante Louise went to answer it.

When Mutti stood there, by my bed, it was so like my many dreams that for a time she didn't seem real. Then Jutta opened the blackout shutters, and suddenly the room was full of sunshine and bird song, and I knew what it felt like to be crying for joy.

67

XI. FOR JUTTA - 8 APRIL 1945

Jutta, isn't it strange: no sooner am I away from you than I have this great urge to talk to you... as though the last eighty-five days had never happened. So once again, I'm giving you a blow by blow account of what's happening to me, without any chance of actually posting my letters in this wild time. When – and where – will we meet?

Yes, I did notice that Tante Louise was crying when we said good-bye, and that you too had tears in your eyes, but – sorry! – it didn't bother me one bit. It didn't make me feel sad for myself, nor sorry for you, nor even guilty at feeling neither of these things. I was just so glad to get away from you all. Even from Schwarzenberg itself, though I hadn't known that I had any strong feelings about the place: when our train had extricated itself from the claustrophobic mountains, it was as if suddenly everything became lighter and brighter. The countryside looked so fresh and peaceful in the spring sunshine. It was only mildly irritating when we were held up outside Leipzig because of an air raid. The noise of the bombs in the distance was ghastly, but as it was broad daylight – and such a lovely day at that – I found it impossible to take the air raid seriously. Well, and, I suppose, because I was so happy. I even found the sight of the bombers beautiful, when they had finished their business and flew away, right over us, all calm and confident in neat formation, almost like wild geese flying over the peat bog in Mickelau.

When they had gone, we expected to continue our journey. But no. We hung around for ages. Eventually, the news spread that there wasn't a station left in Leipzig for us to go to, so we had to walk. Imagine, us with all our clobber! As you know, I had whittled down my own possessions to a minimum when we travelled from Bautzen to Schwarzenberg (and I have regrets only about my lucky horseshoe from Mickelau). But that table linen that Mutti had insisted on reclaiming was like lead weights. I had the feeling that my arms stretched and stretched until they dragged along the ground like a cartoon monkey's.

After more than an hour, a kind lorry driver picked us up and drove us through the smouldering ruins of Leipzig. The smell of rubble and scorched wood was everywhere, and the sun peered without rays through clouds of smoke and dust, like a ghostly orange moon. One of the men on the back of the lorry took great pleasure in pointing to a bright blaze a few streets away and saying, "That's where you might have been, that's the railway station." I held onto the side of the truck, and its vibrations made my knees go wobbly.

After about half an hour's journey by lorry we caught another train that had been forced to turn back in the north of the city. The memory of Leipzig railway station in flames made me quite jumpy whenever we came to a town – and, I think, Mutti too, though neither of us said a word about it.

It was dark when we arrived in Stendal. End of journey, they said, everybody get out. We did, onto a poorly lit platform that was already cram-full with people. No one knew which way to go, so everybody shoved in different directions. Suddenly, all lights went out. Panic. Women screamed, children cried, people lashed out all round them. You couldn't choose where to go, you were carried along by whoever pushed hardest. There was a woman near us who whirled round and round like a spinning top, flailing her arms to keep a clear space for the two small children at her feet. Mutti told me later about someone she had met on the trek who had lost both her children in a panicking crowd: the baby got squashed to death, and the five-year-old was separated from his mother. She didn't know where he'd disappeared to and was nearly out of her mind searching for him. No wonder Mutti now clutched my arm so tightly that it hurt.

Somehow the rumour spread that our old train – the one we'd just got out of – was going on after all, although nobody knew where to. We found ourselves being pushed back into a compartment. It was eerie, as though we had suddenly stepped into a cave full of invisible bodies. Although the platform had seemed dark, there must have been some light, compared with the pitch-blackness of this carriage: all the windows were boarded up, allowing not even a glimmer of stars to show. Suddenly, a sharp tak-tak-tak noise, followed by the sound of splintering glass further up the train, and then prolonged screams. An attack by low-flying aircraft. We were lucky that the damage to the windows in our compartment had been done on an earlier occasion!

It seemed an eternity before the train at last jerked into motion. We were past caring in which direction it went; anywhere away from this inferno was an improvement...

In the morning, we stopped once again in open country, waiting for an air raid over the town of Uelzen to get over and done with. There was a whole tangle of railway tracks coming together at this point, and trains were held up at each line. Passengers were lying among the shrubs on the embankments, sunbathing. Mutti and I joined them. Somebody told us that a train which stood some way behind ours was the one going to Hamburg. What luck, we thought, we can change trains here and now; for we were supposed to be heading that way.

I decided to go and investigate and reserve us two seats. I sauntered off, singing and picking a little bunch of coltsfoot and lamb's tails, just for the joys of spring. One of those bomber squadrons flew over us from the direction of Uelzen, so I thought they had obviously done their damage already. But for some reason, they turned in a wide circle above us. And then it was as though I was watching the newsreel in the cinema, as a string of bombs came plopping out of the planes' bellies. The only thing was, one of the bombs looked a lot bigger than any had done on the cinema screen, and it came closer and closer towards me. I wasn't at all frightened, more astonished. And it wasn't a conscious decision that made me fling myself nose down into the grass. Maybe it was the whoosh of air blowing me over. When, after a bit, I looked up again, there was a bomb crater just ahead of me.

Again, it wasn't a conscious decision to abandon my search for the Hamburg train, and to go back to Mutti instead, but somehow my legs seemed to do it, very fast, stumbling over tussocks and clods of soil. Further away, there was a woman on an embankment, silhouetted against the sky, and she was yelling, yelling, yelling like a maniac. And when I came closer, I could hear that what she yelled was MarleneMarleneMarleneMarlene... I waved my arms and shouted back to her, "Mutti, I'm here, I'm coming..." But she looked over the top of me, her face all wild, and she didn't hear me above the sound of her own voice.

Getting up that embankment was as hard as climbing a rock face in a nightmare. I was dead slow at it. The stupid thing was, I was still clutching that bunch of flowers, all limp and crushed by now, so I flung it away. Then, at last, I reached Mutti, and I hugged her tight until she calmed down. We swore that, come what may, we'd stick close together from then on.

And so we did. We hitched lifts in lorries and cars, we spent a night in the waiting room of a village railway station, sleeping on the table. We even found another train in operation, but it only went from one village to the next. Of course, I hadn't a clue where we were in relation to where we wanted to end up, but Mutti assured me that we were getting closer all the time. In Zeven, we left our luggage in a cafe and walked the last eight kilometres. And in this fashion we arrived in Freyersen at last, a bit footsore and bedraggled, but all in one piece. And Anneli was there to welcome me into my new home.

XII. FOR JUTTA - 10 APRIL 1945

One look at that room which is supposed to be home, and I almost expected to hear a voice saying, "Sorry, full up. Standing room only." Imagine the whole of Mickelau condensed into an area the size of my bedroom. Not only was all the floor space taken up, but things were stacked high against the walls, with just a gap on one side for a small window. Talk about claustrophobia among the Erz mountains! Here, there seemed to be no air to breathe...

The worst thing was that it wasn't the Mickelau chests and curtains that caught the eye, but other people's ugly cast-offs: a huge dark brown bed, very high off the ground and almost square, piled to the ceiling with pillows and eiderdowns. One of those ornate plush sofas – purple! – with the arms worn through and, as I discovered later, with springs that stick into your bum if you sit in the wrong place. Hanging above it, an enormous picture: purple sunset over purple heather, a waterfall standing stagnant on a bed of rocks, the shape of a stag, like a cardboard cut-out, stuck behind a juniper bush – all of it enclosed in a wide mottled gilt frame. I wanted to shut my eyes to it but, on the contrary, could hardly look away – like when you can't stop singing a tune that you hate.

You have to sidle into the room, dodging between trunks and boxes and bundles, and every time you want to change position, you set off a general movement among everyone, like in a barn dance.

Typical farmhouses near Freyersen, Lower Saxony

Still, I don't seriously mind being cramped. I'm too glad to be with Mutti and Anneli again. And Vitya, lovely cuddly Vitya...

The Mosins are the only Mickelau people here – if you can call them that, when they only lived in Mickelau for two months as refugees (as we now live in Freyersen; will that make us Freyersen people in two months?). Volodya and Opa share a chicken hut with another Russian refugee on a nearby farm in this village, and Vitya lives with us. He's grown up a lot: he's quite round and podgy, and he waddles when he moves. His hair isn't stubbly any longer, but sleek and dark, almost black like Volodya's. Of course, he can't remember me, but luckily he isn't shy: he talks and talks, and you can't tell any longer that he isn't German, except that he still speaks Russian to Opa and Volodya.

Frau Brinkmann and family

I would have liked to crawl into my new burrow and just stay there. But Mutti said she had to introduce me to the Brinkmann family, our hosts. Hosts? Well, the owners of the farm on whom we have been dumped willy-nilly.

So she led the way along the corridor from our room, and straight into their kitchen. It's very like our Mickelau kitchen: a large range in one corner, and a long scrubbed wooden table under the window. And there we found the family, sitting on benches round that table – no cloth, no napkins, no nothing... And a saucepan and frying pan standing bang in the middle. What's more, they were eating meat and potatoes from soup bowls. I felt quite embarrassed for them and expected them to jump up and hide at least the pans. But they weren't in the least bit bothered. They went on shovelling in the food, while I walked round shaking each one of them by the hand and performing my best regulation curtsy before Herr and Frau Brinkmann. That seemed to amuse one of the little boys no end. I saw him snigger and nudge his brother, and I felt a great urge to tweak his big sticking-out ears. Am I too old for curtsies? Probably. I felt foolish doing them, anyway, but knowing that Mutti likes that sort of polite gesture, I didn't want to let her down.

They're a big family, the Brinkmanns, in more senses than one: two adults and five children, although the eldest is away in the army now. Frau Brinkmann is huge – not fat exactly, but massive, like the oaken chest she showed me on a later occasion, where they keep their daughter's dowry! Piles of boring sheets and towels; and yet the girl is barely older than me. Fifteen, so Mutti tells me, although to look at her you'd think she was a woman – very like her mum: large bosom, large bum, permed blond hair pressed in tight waves round her shiny moon face. But a bright smile that makes her look more like a child's painting of the sun. Her brother Hannes, who is twelve, is also big, blond and round-faced. The boy with the pot-handle ears is called Werner, but they pronounce it Vairner. That sounds quite pointed and angular, doesn't it? And so is he, skinny almost,

72

and his nose like a badger's. Then there's a snotty-nosed toddler called Günter. He yelled like mad when I tried to shake his hand. Maybe he thought I was trying to wrench his sticky spoon away from him...

Herr Brinkmann looks the nicest: friendly grey eyes, and his handshake was firm as if he meant it. The others' hands all hung limp; Mutti says that's because it isn't their custom to shake hands.

Funny what a lot of differences there are in customs between different parts of Germany. And language, too. Remember how Onkel Rudi used to keep us in stitches with his Dresden accent whenever he came to East Prussia – and then, blow me, didn't they all talk like that in Bautzen! And Anneli's friend Rita of the National Labour Service camp, with her Hamburg way of s-tumbling over s-tick and s-tone? That's how they talk here. And every vowel is pronounced separately. So the Brinkmanns' daughter is called Mari-anne, and she's about to have her Konfirmati-on. When they are amongst themselves, they talk plattdeutsch[16] – even quite posh people, not just the labourers like in Mickelau. It's a different language from the East Prussian version, and has to be learnt like English or Russian. Mutti can't understand a word of it!

Frau Brinkmann kept marvelling at the fact that Mutti had managed to get me here. She went on and on about how she'd never believed Mutti would make it, never! To get all the way to Schwarzenberg alive, in spite of the bombing all over the place; and back again, too! The more she talked, the more I began to feel like the man in the poem who had, without knowing it, ridden right across Lake Constance as it lay hidden under a covering of snow; and when he was told what danger he had passed through, he dropped down dead. Luckily I escaped even that fate – but only just!

*It's silly to keep comparing Freyersen with Mickelau, but I can't help it. I suppose it's because I've somehow thought about coming here as **coming home**. And it's so very, very different... Remember the game we used to play of describing people in terms of something else – animals, flowers, books? Well, if I had to describe Mickelau as a story, it would be a fairy tale about elves and rainbows and flower people. Freyersen would be an old folk tale of ancient gods and giants and thunder. Mickelau is birch trees: tall, graceful, silvery-green, or golden in autumn, or frosty-white. Freyersen is oaks: solid, dark, gnarled, and the houses huddled close among them as if for protection.*

Just about every house in this village is of the same type. You must have seen pictures of it in calendars of "Our Beautiful Fatherland": a thick thatched roof hanging low over very wide half-timbered red brick walls. The oaken beams are set in symmetrical squares, stained black with creosote, and the brick work of the posh houses is painted dark red with – guess what – ox blood! The Brinkmanns' is plain brick colour. At one gable end, there is a wooden edge to the thatch that ends in a cross of two carved horses' heads at the very top. That's to ward off the evil spirits, and it's the symbol of Lower Saxony. Mutti says they need it.

---

[16] the local dialect

At the same gable end, there's a huge broad wooden double door leading into the house. It's big enough for a full hay cart to drive through, and that's exactly what it's meant for: inside, there's a church-sized aisle in which two hay carts can stand nose to tail, and all the roof space above is hay loft. To either side of this central aisle are the stables – cowsheds to the left, and two loose-boxes for calves and horses to the right. The Brinkmanns have six dairy cows (Friesians) with homely names like Ella and Dora written up in wonky letters above their stands, not impersonal stud book registration numbers, say 43/4, like in Mickelau. The Brinkmanns have only one horse, a dark brown Hanoverian. It's used for pulling the cart and for ploughing, not for riding! Nobody in the village rides on horseback, although I'm told that Hanoverians make good mounts and take part in all sorts of international show jumping competitions. They're more coarse-limbed than the Trakehner, but quite good-looking.

What about our Mickelau horses, you ask. Well, that's a subject that reduces Mutti to tears of misery and rage in turns. Anger mostly on behalf of "Illyrier". He was the first to go.

It happened during those grim days when they were caught up in the bottle neck near the Vistula. A ferry was to take them across the river to what they all then thought was safety. Blizzards were blowing, the road was blocked with big snow drifts, and, to top it all, news spread that the ferry had broken down. Lots of people abandoned their vehicles and plodded along on foot with what luggage they could carry; mostly women and children and old men, of course. But there were also a few young men in soldiers' uniforms who laughed and made jokes about saying Heil Hitler with **both** hands up.

Mutti's trek was among those that decided to stick it out. Four whole days and nights they stayed there, huddled up in fur coats and blankets and shawls with temperatures of -30 °C and lower. Anneli says they all looked like scarecrows, because their arms stuck out sideways with that many clothes! They protected the horses, too, as best they could, with sacking and rugs. They scrounged firewood and coal and bales of hay from a nearby farm, and set up a sort of gypsy encampment on the road. Anneli even took out her accordion and played tunes for people to sing to. And although they were cold and hungry and scared of what would happen, they almost enjoyed themselves in a funny kind of way.

At one point, a couple of Russian tanks appeared in the distance, stopped and set down a dozen or so passengers, then turned and vanished from sight. The passengers – families from a village further back – had a strange tale to tell. They had chosen to stay at home and wait for the Russian invasion. They had searched out their long-hidden Communist Party membership cards, and when the tanks rolled in, had waved these in the air like certificates of immunity. But one of the tank crew who spoke German had shouted at them to get out quick: Soviet soldiers were in no mood for friendship, they killed and raped in revenge for what had happened during the German occupation in Russia. And then these very Soviet soldiers had given them a lift to catch up with the throng of refugees. No wonder they felt confused.

On another day, a German NCO suddenly turned up from nowhere. He'd shot out his arm under Mutti's nose in a Hitler salute and attempted to click his heels *in all that snow, really ridiculous. Mutti and Anneli nearly got the giggles, but they sensed something threatening in him. His eyes kept roving between Mutti and Illyrier ("and he managed a lecherous sideways look at Anneli as well", Mutti says). "I confiscate your horse," he barked, and made for Illyrier. But Mutti stopped him in his tracks. "By what right?" she wanted to know, "Where is your requisition order?"*

*Imagine, our gentle, accommodating Mutti! Anneli says she stood by, speechless with admiration. "Well," says Mutti, "I could tell he was lying, the scoundrel: he was on the run like the rest of them, but he was too cowardly even to admit it. **And** he wanted a nice bit of booty to take home from the wars!"*

The man had pulled a scruffy piece of paper out of his pocket and scribbled on it, "One horse plus saddle for use of the Great German Army, unit such and such", and an illegible scrawl of a signature. That really made Mutti wild. No, not the fact that you couldn't read his name: the offending word was "horse". "Will you kindly replace that with ONE PEDIGREE TRAKEHNER STALLION", she told him acidly, and added under her breath, "I hope he throws you for that!" Cheered by that prospect, both she and Anneli had bitten back their tears to watch Illyrier buck in rebellion against the unknown rider. Unfortunately, the whirling snow swallowed them up while the man was still hanging on to Illyrier's mane for dear life!

And yet, the poor wretch, if only he'd known Mutti, he would have said to her, "Look, I'm scared stiff, will you help me get home to my Mummy?" And she would have been all concern and sympathy. But as it is, she still rages against him and takes good care of that scrap of paper because, she says, "One of these days I'll claim compensation..." But really, I think she knows that the receipt is no more than a souvenir of that terrible time.

She has also kept a careful record of the various places where they had to abandon one or other of our horses who became too weak or lame to continue the journey. They are dotted along the whole 1000-odd kilometre route like staging posts from the old coaching days. Mutti says we'll pick them up on our way back home. I'm not sure if she believes that herself.

Only four of our Trakehners and the Mosins' tough little pony made it all the way to Freyersen. As none of the farmers in the village have space for spare horses, they are billeted in separate farms several kilometres away from here. Mutti has never-ending wrangles with these farmers who want to buy them for what Mutti calls a pittance and they call an overgenerous offer. They have us in their power, worse luck, for it will be our loss if they neglect the horses.

Right next to the Brinkmanns' cowshed, there's a bit partitioned off as a kind of dairy: a wooden bench with room for three milk churns at most, and nails on the walls to hang up filters and funnels and measures, that's all. Our head dairyman would have had a fit at such a primitive set-up.

And next to that, a room that's hardly different from the loose boxes except for the furnishings: a bed and a chair. That's where the farm hand lives. At present, he too is an East Prussian refugee.

If you come into the house by the side door from the farm yard, you step straight into what the Brinkmanns call the "wash-room": a slightly sloping concrete floor with a drainage hole, and a concrete trough by a water pump. That's where all the Brinkmanns wash. Imagine it: you come into the house, all unsuspecting, to be confronted by Frau Brinkmann's dangling boobs! I think the Brinkmanns are shocked that we prefer sloshing water round our overcrowded room for the sake of privacy...

You reach the human part of the house (are farm hands not human?) by walking through the frosted glass door at the inner end of the hay cart aisle into the kitchen. We are warned always to shut that door, to lessen the likelihood of mice nipping through. Nice prospect for Mutti! The kitchen is the Brinkmanns' main living room. Their "parlour" is the mirror image of our room, and even the furniture is similar to the stuff they gave us, only newer. It even includes a heather landscape over a plush sofa! The Brinkmanns only use this room for special visitors on feast days. Apart from that, they have three tiny bedrooms – one for the parents and Günter (one bed for the three of them to share), one for Marianne, and one for the two middle-sized boys (one bed). So you can see, they don't exactly live in a palace, and it isn't surprising that they resent us. But then, we aren't here by choice, either...

You'll think I've forgotten to mention the loo. I haven't, but it is part of the pig sty, another picturesque heart-in-the-door affair. To get to it, we have to walk through the Brinkmanns' kitchen, into the stable part, through the wash-room, and out into the little yard. The pigsty stands at right angles to the main house, and the privy stands alongside it, modestly turning its back on the house, which means that you get an uninterrupted view of the village street when you are enthroned there (the smell usually forces you to leave the door open!). I imagine in winter it must be a good deal colder even than the privy in Ebersbach, what with not being an integral part of the pigsty. But that's not our problem. In six months' time we must surely have a permanent home of our own...

The big wooden beam across the gable end of all the houses is carved with a religious verse in elaborate gothic letters, beautifully picked out in white paint. The one on the Brinkmanns' house reads, "Lord take care of all this, take care of my house; and of all my kin who go in and out." Mutti says that definitely doesn't include us.

XIII. FOR JUTTA - 30 APRIL 1945

Well, we are under British occupation now. I've seen my first Englishman, in fact the village is swarming with them – all in baggy khaki uniform that doesn't look the least bit military. I like it for that reason. It gives the soldiers the appearance of big harmless teddy bears. I don't know if Vamir would agree with me!

And who, I hear you ask, is Vamir? He is Rita's boyfriend; remember the famous Rita from Hamburg with her s-trange way of s-peaking? A few days after I arrived in Freyersen, there was a phone call for us. They have a good system in Freyersen: one farmer (it happens to be the Brinkmanns) has a telephone in their parlour which everybody can use, like at a post office; and outside callers can ring this number and leave messages to be taken to any house in the village. Our call was from Rita: could she and Vamir, a Brazilian student, come and hide with us until the end of the war? Apparently the Gestapo were rounding up all kinds of foreigners in Hamburg, and Vamir feared for his life. Well, you know Mutti! Of course, she agreed – though how she could be so confident that two more bodies could fit into our room, I do not know. Already we slept three to a bed (Mutti, Vitya and me) and Anneli curled up on the short spiky sofa, and not a square centimetre of spare space in sight. But we stacked chairs and boxes onto the table to make room for Rita to sleep on the floor, and the Brinkmanns allowed Vamir to sleep in the corridor outside our room. We've rescued plenty of bedding from Mickelau, so that was no problem. No one told the Brinkmanns the true reason for Rita's visit: we said they were afraid of the bombing raids on Hamburg.

*How romantic, you'll say, hiding a Brazilian! I thought so too, at first. But Vamir was a disappointment. He was pale and pimply and not in the least foreign looking, and he behaved like any selfish and opinionated pipsqueak. He sat back with a look of suffering on his face, expecting us to dance in attendance. His only contribution to our welfare was to assure Mutti again and again of his undying gratitude. "When our Anglo-American liberators come," he kept saying, "I will give you a beautiful dinner service." (I suppose he picked on that because our chipped china and cracked plastic offended his dignity?) The trouble was that our "liberators" had the liberation of Vamir low on their list of priorities: they by-passed us and headed for Berlin, giving Vamir time to build up at least **my** expectations: was it to be gold leaf Meissen, or dragon-patterned Rosenthal?*

19 April was a lovely sunny day. Marianne Brinkmann offered to take us for a walk to the woods to see if the wild lilies-of-the-valley were in bloom. I couldn't go because I had tonsillitis. But I wasn't sorry: the chances of being alone are so rare and precious. So I lay there on the big princess-on-the-pea tower of bedding, thinking deep thoughts and staring at the lampshade on the ceiling (we were on the same level): a white china affair with pink roses, and a fringe of tiny green glass beads. Suddenly there was a loud bang, and the bead fringe tinkled like wind-bells in the film of "The Land of Smiles". And then, less loud but obviously closer, a sharp burst of "tak-tak-tak". Before I could sort out what was happening, all the others were back in the room: they had seen British tanks on the main road.

We stayed huddled together and waited. Then came the rumour that British troops were in the village. Vamir rushed out, jubilantly waving his arms. I watched him slantways through the window, as he bore down on a group of khaki soldiers. A second later, Vamir lay prostrate on the ground! One of the soldiers (it turned out later that he was a professional boxer) had landed him a neat right hook and knocked him down. The next thing was that Vamir was led away – not, as I had come to expect, in triumph on the soldiers' shoulders, but ignominiously, to be locked up. Why, asked the British, was this man still free unless he was in league with the Gestapo? (Of course, the reason was that Brazil had only recently changed sides in the war.) Poor Vamir. Well, it was soon sorted out, and he was set free – I think because it stuck out a mile that he is utterly insignificant. But from then on he was limp like a punctured balloon.

So we didn't get our dinner set. But, as things developed, Vamir was able to do us one good turn. The Brinkmanns' farmhouse was taken over by the Red Cross for their headquarters, and all of us, including the Brinkmanns, were turfed out. You might think that after nearly six months' practice of living on the road, this would be child's play for us. But in fact, it was easier for the Brinkmanns: they moved in with relations at the other end of the village, and what they didn't take with them, they locked up in cupboards and storerooms.

As for us, the only offer of a roof over our heads came from the Mosins in their chicken hutch (in case you misunderstand: the chickens had been moved out in March when the Mosins moved in). The trouble was that the hut was hardly big enough for nine people to lie down at the same time, let alone store any of our belongings. Vamir complained to the British Military Authority about their undignified treatment of him, their Brazilian ally, so luckily they gave him and Rita permission to stay in our room at the Brinkmanns.

That left just seven of us – the three Mosins, another Russian refugee called Adam, and Mutti, Anneli and me – for the chicken hut. Anneli once said that life could never be really bad for us because we knew how to make the best of things. That certainly applied to our week's stay at the chicken hut. Under her initiative, we rolled up our bedding in the day time to make a sort of Roman couch. A suitcase laid flat and covered with a headscarf became a table, and on it stood the old tooth mug with wild flowers as a symbol of civilization.

Anneli was the only person in the village with any reasonable knowledge of English, so off and on she had to act as interpreter. Both of us enjoyed practising our English and were glad when the soldiers talked to us. My first new phrase was, "No fraternization", which the soldiers said jokingly, but with a furtive glance over their shoulders. It reminded me of our contact with the Russian prisoners at home! I wonder where they are... One of the British soldiers showed us a picture of Russian and American soldiers shaking hands as the two armies met at Torgau by the river Elbe.

There was one particularly friendly man who started chatting to us and asked if we liked chocolate. Well, to be honest, he asked Anneli if she liked chocolate. When she hesitated, I chipped in fast, greed overcoming my inhibitions: "Oh yes, I like!"

78

He promised to bring us some later on. "Wasn't he kind!" I said, and waited for him all day.

That night, when we were already bedded down in our chicken hut, like sardines in a tin, there was a loud knock. Here was the chocolate as promised, said a voice. "Hurrah!" I exclaimed, and made for the door. Mutti nearly went berserk, and Anneli yelled at me not to be so naïve, for heaven's sake! And then she shouted at Volodya, urging him to "say something!" "What?" he asked, puzzled – understandably so, in my opinion. After all, he doesn't speak English.

"Something! Anything! But loud and aggressive!" Anneli said. Poor Volodya. And him the gentlest of people! I kept imploring Anneli to tell the soldier to leave the chocolate by the door, but she jeered and said, he never came to bring chocolate, not at this hour! And yet she is the one who keeps talking about how one should always expect the best of people.

Well, I said no more, but inwardly I hoped that I would prove her wrong. In the morning, I made sure I was the first to go outside. But it was like waking up on Advent Sunday and not finding a present in your slipper. Even more shattering was the fact that when I next saw this soldier, he behaved as if he didn't know me. Maybe I **am** too naïve?

XIV. FOR JUTTA - 8 MAY 1945

So this is the end of the war: an announcement on the Brinkmanns' radio that Friedeburg, Stump and Keitel have signed our unconditional surrender. Who are these people? Had you ever heard of them before? I hadn't, and nobody here seems to know anything about them. Perhaps that's appropriate: insignificant people to match my own indifferent reaction.

I expect you heard about Hitler having "died a hero's death". According to rumours that the Brinkmanns have come across, he and his sweetheart Eva Braun committed suicide in their Berlin bunker. Hardly heroic! Not that I care one way or the other...

I'm more concerned about what's happened to Väti and Claus. We must surely get news of them. Although I've always argued that certainty is better than ignorance, when it comes to the point I'm not so sure. As long as you don't know, you can at least go on hoping...

So it's really not all that odd that I'm not skipping about, shouting for joy. Of course I'm glad that the hateful war is over, and that there is an end to the fighting and killing... but only when I make myself think about it. I'm certainly not miserable, like Frau Brinkmann seems to be, on the "We've-lost-the-war" lines. It's just that now that this longed-for event has happened, it strikes me as quite unimportant.

Peace. The word suggests a return to normality, and for lots of people it will be just that. But what on earth is normal for us? Frau Brinkmann rubs salt in our wounds, not from cruelty but because she is so stupid. "Thank God, you can go back to your own home now," she said. As if you can just wipe your hands on your apron and say, "So that's the end of that little job, now we can carry on living as before we were so rudely interrupted..."

When Mutti burst out crying, Frau Brinkmann looked all huffy. I bet she thinks we don't want to leave her precious Freyersen. If only she knew how we long for Mickelau! But I can't see the remotest chance of us returning there. Whatever changes this peace brings, can you imagine the Russians allowing the Germans to get East Prussia back? I can't.

So what will happen to us? Do we go on living forever in nine square metres of space, all four of us (Mutti, Anneli, Vitya and me)? And on what? What work can Mutti possibly do? Can you imagine her as a farm labourer on the Brinkmanns' fields? Anneli, yes, she'll manage to get a proper job. She is so good at English, she gets asked more and more often to act as interpreter. But sometimes I think Mutti and I are really unfair to her: we cling to her as though it is her duty to take care of us, and whenever she shows signs of wanting an independent life, we turn nasty. I know it, but I can't stop myself... because I feel so helpless. What can I do to support Mutti?

Now, suddenly, I understand why Väti was so anxious for me to get some sort of education. Well, I suppose that will be one of the aspects of peace: back to school. I can't say I fancy the idea. After nearly a year without, I feel too old for that game. But at least I do see the importance of it now: to equip me for earning my living, as Väti said.

The only thing I'm good at so far is doing odd jobs for the Brinkmanns, for which they pay me as they see fit: a few eggs, a handful of potatoes, or a free meal with them. Not exactly a living wage, but useful. What's more, I enjoy the work enormously, even though it's very different from working on the land in Mickelau.

Here, the farmers all live together in a village – about twenty of them in Freyersen – with their fields scattered round about: a strip of arable here, a meadow there, some fenced-in pasture somewhere else. I have no idea how they can tell each other's plots apart. The fields are so small that it isn't worth using a lot of machinery. Only one of the farmers has a tractor, and so they call him "tractor-Mayer". The Brinkmanns have just the one horse, and many of the jobs that were done mechanically with horse-drawn implements at home are done by hand.

Planting potatoes, for example: you walk along a newly-ploughed furrow with a basket of seed potatoes under your arm. You drop your potatoes in front of you, neatly spaced, and, as you move forward, you tread on each one, so as to lodge it firmly in the soil. Then a new furrow is ploughed which covers up the previous one. When I walk home at the end of the day, I still put one foot in front of the other as though I had potatoes to tread in.

I've also learnt what they call "Schiethumpel utsmieten". (I think I told you that they speak their own version of Plattdeutsch here nearly all the time.) Translated, it means "scattering shit heaps". Not just cow muck either: every so often it is the contents of the "thunder box". Just think what we wasted in Mickelau by having a flush toilet. I needn't tell you how I smell after that sort of activity. It's quite a job getting cleaned up in a bowlful of water amongst all our clobber in our dining/sitting/bed/bathroom/kitchen. (Bathrooms are as rare as tractors, and the fact that Frau Brinkmann's sister has one is talked of with awe and respect.)

The problem of washing away the smells also applies to another newly acquired skill of mine: milking. I feel extraordinarily proud of the fact that I manage to coax anything out of the cows' udders, and aim it into the bucket. But I reek of sour milk nearly all the time, and you can imagine how I hate that. So that puts me off a permanent career as milk maid. What can I do instead? I have absolutely no idea. No wonder I feel so anxious at the beginning of this new peace time.

XV. FOR JUTTA - 10 SEPTEMBER 1945

Vitya is dead. Four years old, and dead. Volodya said, "Why God play with me like cat with mouse?" And I must say, I see his point: Vitya escaped when the Soviet partisans killed most of his family because of their involvement with the German occupation; he escaped from the Soviet army when the Germans retreated; first as far as Mickelau, and then, after barely two months of settled life there, on again, through the horrors of that winter trek of which I know so little, except that Mutti still shudders at the very mention of it.

Vitya survived it all, blizzards and rain, lack of food and shelter, without even becoming ill. And then, at the end of the war, the Mosins were threatened by the new danger of being returned to Russia against their will, because Stalin claimed that all Russian citizens in Germany should be repatriated. Each time there was a rumour of Soviet officials on the prowl in our area, Volodya and Opa used to hide in the Brinkmanns' hay loft. But just recently, the Canadian government had offered asylum to all the "Displaced Persons" who did not want to return home to Communist countries, and so the Mosins were given permission to emigrate. A new beginning. And now, barely two weeks later, Vitya is dead.

At the end of August, the Mosins were moved to a Displaced Persons' camp at Heidenau, about twenty kilometres from Freyersen. That was bad enough for us, being separated from Vitya like that. But at least we thought it was for his own good...

I went to visit the Mosins at their camp on 1 September. As soon as I saw Volodya, I knew that something ghastly had happened: his skin looked grey, and his eyes were sunk in dark hollows. Vitya had scarlet fever and diphtheria, and had been taken away to an isolation hospital. Volodya and I set out to visit him there.

The hospital was twenty-two kilometres from the camp, and we had to go there on foot. Volodya walked so fast, I almost had to run to keep up with him. It was very hot and, as usual nowadays, my shoes were rubbing.

The nurse at the hospital was cool and official and said nobody could see "Viktor", not even his father. Volodya tried to plead with her, but his German came out all muddled, and he kept looking at me as though he hoped I would persuade her to change her mind. But I didn't know what to say.

As a concession, the nurse led us to the window of the ward where Vitya lay. I wish she hadn't. His podgy little hand was hanging limp between the bars of his cot, and he was whimpering softly. Just like when he played his favourite game of "Dead Dog", pretending to be "kaputt". Only this time it wasn't pretend...

The road back to the camp was very straight and hard, and my feet were burning with pain. Volodya, by my side, was crying.

When Anneli went to visit Vitya two days later, she was told that he was dead. He had died the day before, and nobody had bothered to let his father know. Now I can't get rid of the feeling that it was my fault. I should have told the nurse to take extra care of Vitya, I should have persuaded her to let Volodya hold him and comfort him. Unlike Volodya, I had the language with which to do it – and yet I hadn't got the words out...

We were told that his heart was too weak to stand up to his illness. Mutti says that's because of his unnatural childhood, with hardly any time to run about and play. He had spent nearly a quarter of his whole life sitting still on a pony cart, travelling across the whole of Europe from the Urals to the North Sea...

The day of the funeral was even hotter than that of my visit to the hospital. The air flickered before my eyes as we walked to the cemetery behind the tiny coffin. It made me feel giddy. You know how some people think of chrysanthemums as funeral flowers: from now on I shall always think of heather in that way. The whole countryside smelt of it, and the cemetery was like a heather garden: blue-black juniper bushes stood there, like people in mourning. The humps of new graves – so many! – broke like boils through the ground cover of lings and bell heathers. Where we stopped with our little procession, that boil seemed still to be festering – a mound of peaty soil beside such a deep and narrow crater... Here, the coffin was opened according to Russian custom. Volodya and Opa went up to it and bent over to kiss Vitya. Anneli did, too. I wanted to, but couldn't: I think I was afraid that death might be catching.

Death. The horrid sickly smell of it. That was all I could remember about the time when Oma Wiemer died and I secretly crept into her room to have a peep at her, lying there by candle light, yellow and motionless. And when her room became my bedroom, I imagined for ages that the smell lingered in the bed. And I remember thinking that I was the only one who cared about her death, for all the many wreaths with their long inscribed silk ribbons...

Anneli and Claus and all the visiting cousins saw her only as the nagging old woman who criticized our table manners and dirty fingernails, and they enjoyed playing tricks on her, like nudging the sofa to watch her head wobble from side to side as she sat there by the stove. But I knew her from cosy afternoons in her room, when she used to hold out her two closed fists at me and ask, "Odds or evens?" Inside were lumps of candied sugar, like splinters of glass, and I would get either a big handful or a measly few, depending on the luck of my call. The sugar was for putting into coffee. Despite Mutti's disapproval, Oma always let me drink her strong coffee, from a tiny green glass cup with bobbly white and pink flowers on it. How I resented Tante Louise going off with that cup after Oma's death!

I missed Opa Wiemer, too, when he died – but I was a bit relieved at the same time, because it meant an end to the ordeal of good-night kisses from that rough bushy moustache that nearly always had the remains of supper hanging in it.

I was kept away from those two funerals: death, like the mating of horses, was not for the eyes of children. But I watched the procession going along the drive, across the main road and on to the farm cemetery in the midst of open fields: the group of mourners in black following the carriage that was covered in a huge pile, wreaths in beautiful floral arrangements. It was all so solemn and sad, I was glad not to be part of it.

Oma's and Opa's Golden Wedding

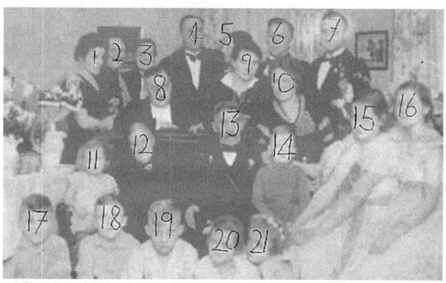

1 Tante Anne, 2 Tante Trudchen, 3 Omi (Hahn), 4 Väti. 5 Mutti, 6 Onkel Kurt (Wiemer),
7 Onkel Egon (Kowalewski), 8 Onkel Bruno (Wiemer), 9 Tante Gretel (Wiemer),
10 Tante (Frieda) Louise (Kowalewski), 11 Gudrun (Wiemer), 12 Oma, 13 Opa,
14 Ulrich (Wiemer), 15 Anneli, 16 Lore (Kowalewski),
17 Rolf "Mops" (Wiemer), 18 Frank (Wiemer), 19 Claus, 20 Jutta, 21 Marlene

I would have been glad, too, not to go to Halina Biernacki's funeral. But Mutti thought in this case that it was important for us all to attend as a sign of our sympathy. Although the Biernackis, like all the Polish families in the district, were supposed to be friendly immigrants rather than enemies, the Party administration refused permission for the other Poles to come to the funeral. But they came anyway, in little groups cross-country, avoiding the roads. It was like an invasion of unearthly creatures. I had never realized before just how many Poles there were in our neighbourhood.

A Catholic priest came to Mickelau to take the service. I watched him dress in our sitting room: a white tulle surplice over his black gown, a gold-embroidered black shawl smoothed round his neck, a black cap with silk tassels on his head – much more impressive than the Lutheran pastor in his plain black surplice who officiated at our family funerals, but also more unreal, like a film.

The procession from the Biernackis' cottage to the graveyard was led by a man carrying a big wooden crucifix on which the figure of Jesus was impaled. Then came the priest and, behind him, a group of chanting young girls carrying wreaths. The Biernackis had turned down Väti's offer of a carriage for the coffin. Instead, it was carried all the way on the shoulders of men in black suits. At the graveside, the coffin was opened. Halina looked like a doll, with her loose flaxen hair, painted red lips and pink cheeks. When the coffin was lowered into the ground, Frau Biernacki screamed aloud and made to jump in after it. Mutti put her arm round her and tried to comfort her: "Think of your lovely sons..." "I shit on my sons!" she screamed, and I was shocked.

But when the shovels of soil thudded down on Vitya's coffin, I think I understood. I shit on all survivors.

And just at this terrible time the English soldiers decided to get all happy and excited and celebrate the end of the war. Why so late, considering the war ended on 8 May? But they say no, that was only VE day – victory in Europe. The Japanese war went on until 2 September (the very day Vitya died)... Apparently the Americans dropped some wonderful new bombs on Japan. They are called atom bombs, and only two were needed to destroy two whole big towns, Hiroshima and Nagasaki. Just about all the people who lived there died – so many thousands!

If I multiplied how I feel about Vitya a hundred-thousand-fold...

I don't even want to try.

XVI. FOR JUTTA - 8 MAY 1946

It's a year since – I nearly said, "since peace broke out", but that would have been quite the wrong expression for something that has changed life so little for us, and so slowly.

Instead of refugee families going home, as Frau Brinkmann had imagined, there are even more of them arriving in this part of Germany. They are the people from the provinces east of the Oder and the Neisse rivers, which have been given to Poland. Given by whom? The British soldiers here talk about a "Potsdam Agreement" between the Allies. I've learnt a new word for being homeless: "repatriated". That's what has happened to the German population in the new Poland. Some of them have terrible tales to tell of their experiences. So it's a good job, after all, that we escaped when we did.

It took until last October before we heard from Claus, and even then only a printed form with ticks in the appropriate places: "I've been taken prisoner by the British; I am well." That card had been posted in May and had taken five months to reach us. And it wasn't until Christmas that we had a letter from him, and his address: a POW camp in Scotland. Lovely to know he's safe, lovely to be able to write to him. But somehow, half the time I forget to be happy about it.

Still no news from Väti, so we must assume he's dead: other people have had mail from their relatives in Russian prison camps, and a few old men have even been sent home from Russia. Väti had several addresses apart from the Bautzen one for contacting us, and, amazingly, they all survived the war, even Onkel Rudi in Dresden and, of course, Rita in Hamburg. To make doubly sure, Mutti registered our names with the Red Cross as well: they run a "search service" to help missing persons and split-up families to track each other down. No result from them, either. So that's the end of that.

You wonder at me saying it so coldly, me, his favourite "Mausie"? But how else could I say it? At what stage should I have started crying and grieving? The last time I saw him – that day in January 1945 when I was furious with him for sending me away to Bautzen, and he with me for making a fuss? But neither he nor I knew then that we were saying good-bye forever.

Oh, I feel sad all right, more than anyone knows; but not in the way that makes me want to cry; more like a tummy ache deep down inside me. I miss him for all sorts of reasons: I want him to be here, to be in charge, to make everything come right. I want him to take the responsibility off Mutti's shoulders.

Also, I long for him as someone to talk to seriously. Mutti is infuriating in that respect: whenever she and I disagree about something, she stops any argument by saying that I'm "too young to know about such things".

Would Väti have been the same? I'm quite jealous at times when Anneli tells me that Väti thought this and that, and I realize that I don't know him in that way at all. I suppose I was too young then, and he too busy, and he liked me just to relax with. And, of course, I miss him for that, too: the feel of his scratchy cheek and the smell of cigar and outdoors, and of Väti.

At other times, I try to imagine all the terrible ways in which he might have died, and how lonely he must have been, and worried about us all, and then, yes, I do cry. And wish there was some way of reaching him, to tell him we're all right, and to comfort him.

Is he better off dead? It's impossible to imagine him in Freyersen.

When I think of Väti, the picture I get of him is sitting on horseback, very stern and upright, like one of those statues of generals that stand among the ruins in Hamburg. And yet, a general? That was the last thing he was: he was a farmer through and through. And his severity, his fierceness, had all to do with that. He couldn't abide inefficiency, and if he saw it, he lost his temper. More often than not, Claus used to be the object of his wrath.

It was taken for granted by us all that Claus would eventually take over the farm from Väti. Farming tradition demanded that the eldest son stepped into his father's shoes; neither Anneli (by virtue of being the oldest child), nor I (because of my desire to become a farmer) would have dreamt of claiming this privilege for ourselves; nor would it have occurred to Claus to consider any other career for himself. So Väti tried to groom him early into that role.

But Claus was dreamy and lazy and interested only in horses. He did badly at the Secondary School in Insterburg; mainly, I think, because he spent most of his time at the riding school where his skill at handling awkward horses was greatly appreciated. When he came home for weekends, he also skived off to the stables from whatever job Väti had allocated to him. As a result, Väti was constantly irritated by him.

One lunch time has stuck in my mind when, I don't remember for what reason, Väti gave Claus a resounding slap. Claus's head jerked forward with such force that he shattered the plate and cut his nose. Bright crimson blood spurted onto his food. I'm not sure if Claus cried. Mutti, Anneli and I certainly did, and we rushed from the room in different directions. Although I was desperately angry with Väti, I didn't want to hear other people's anger with him.

An even worse example of Väti's temper haunted me since I was about ten years old. He and I were walking along a farm track. It was a working day, and I don't know why Väti wasn't on horseback, which was his usual way of making his rounds of inspection: a horse gave him both greater speed and a higher vantage point. We saw an empty dung cart coming towards us. The man in charge – a Polish labourer new to the farm – was walking alongside the horses, leading them by the reins. The proper way was to sit in the saddle of the horse on the left and control the horse on the right by means of a side strap. "What is this nonsense," Väti muttered, "Walking at snail's pace! I'll teach him, wasting time!"

I read the signs of oncoming wrath and hastily sheered off cross-country, so as not to be part of the scene. But I watched from the distance. I heard Väti's angry voice and then… saw him lash out. Hitting a boy like Claus was one thing, but hitting a grown man! I ran through the fields, crying, and I never wanted to talk to Väti again.

That evening, the Pole came to the house to speak to Väti. The two men had their conversation on the veranda, and I did my best to listen from the hall. "You've got to learn," Väti said, "I can't go chopping and changing for everybody's convenience." And walked off. On the way out, the Pole suddenly grabbed hold of Claus's hand, kissed it and sobbed, "Oh Pan!" A grown man weeping, a grown man calling a mere boy like Claus "Master"! It was too horrible.

But when it came to the new job allocation for the following week, the Pole was relieved of his work with horses. Was it done from pity? Was it done to ensure the smooth progress of work? Or did Mutti have a hand in it?

She was a great advocate for people in trouble. I don't think she was ever bothered about right and wrong: for her, it merely depended on who she was sorry for. So she jumped to the defence of anyone who was in a position of weakness, or looked sad or ill. People on the farm came to her with anything from a cut finger to a broken heart. All the prisoners were objects of her pity, and she showed this by a smile or words of encouragement, and by giving them little gifts of extra food whenever she could. I thoroughly approved, and admired and loved her for it.

She also extended her sympathies to the agricultural apprentices. These were mostly the young sons of farmers who came to us as part of their training before taking over their fathers' farms. Väti was very strict with them, and Mutti automatically took their part against him. So much so that, in the case of Herr Bormann, I became thoroughly worried. I must have been about twelve at the time, and well-read in romantic fiction. Mutti was obviously in love with Herr Bormann; what if she eloped with him? Once the suspicion was there, I found all sorts of proof for it: the way he loitered over a meal, or the way he rushed away from us as soon as the final "Mahlzeit" had been pronounced; the way he looked at Mutti, or the way he didn't look at her. Eventually I could bear it no longer and burst out sobbing, "You don't love Väti any more, you just love Herr Bormann!" It was humiliating that she obviously found this funny – and Väti, too!

Years later in Freyersen I went through a period of jealousy on my own behalf, and confronted Mutti with it: "You love Anneli more than me..." I expected her to deny it, and I would not have believed her. But she said, "I think I always love best the one who at the time needs my love the most. It was Claus in Mickelau, and now it's Anneli." I saw the sense in that: Anneli was, at the time, going through one emotional entanglement after another...

I think everyone in Mickelau loved Mutti. But surprisingly, although people feared Väti, they also respected him. Lebrun, one of the Belgian prisoners, told Anneli how he had heard the Russian prisoners praise him: if only, they would say, we could get him to run one of our state farms! In the months after the war, we gradually managed to make contact with many of our old East Prussian farm labourers. Most of them were living in Soviet-occupied territory, and I expected them to see Väti as the wicked capitalist exploiter of the poor. But they all went out of their way to express their admiration for him – for his efficiency and fair-mindedness.

How could Väti possibly have adjusted to life in lodgings on someone else's poky farm? Though, of course, some men like Väti have managed it.

Onkel Arnold has, in a way. All their family are now safely united in a little village in Holstein, called Blunk. But after what adventures! They make our own look like a holiday excursion.

Omi and Tante Lena and their combined treks left Alischken at the end of January 1945. They got into even worse congestion on the roads than Mutti and Anneli had done, and were directed across the lagoon of the Frische Haff. This was frozen over, but every so often a particularly heavy wagon would break through the ice. So the route had to be changed constantly. When Tante Lena and Omi arrived there, they were given a brand-new track, marked out with stakes in the virgin snow. It was dark by then. So Annelore led the way on foot, carrying a hurricane lantern.

"Just as well we couldn't see any further than the circle of light ahead of us," Tante Lena told us, "We would truly have despaired: broken-down vehicles with all their contents... barouches, sleighs, carts, collapsed horses, and collapsed people, too..."

Well, they got across all right with all their wagons. Horses and people scrabbled up the steep bank onto the Nehrung.

Tante Lena said, "There was this old couple, grey haired, intellectual types – quite incongruous, trudging through the snow with their elegant leather suitcases... I'd have liked to offer them a lift – I regret it still – but how could we? There were so many others, and we were overladen anyway..."

Once they reached the mainland, their progress was similar to that of Mutti's and Anneli's trek. They followed much the same route along the northern coast of Germany, playing cat and mouse with the Red Army, but managing to outpace them. And just as Mutti's trek had been sluiced off to Freyersen in Lower Saxony, they were sent to Blunk in Holstein. They were given a similar little room on a farm for their living quarters.

Onkel Arnold, meanwhile, had to defend Berschienen with his pathetic handful of People's Militia against Russian artillery. He was wounded – stomach wound – dismissed and more or less told to go and find himself a hospital. He managed to persuade his superiors to let his orderly, Franz, go with him: an old dairyman from a neighbouring farm who had collapsed into uncontrollable weeping at the sight of his prostrate master. I can see them, like characters in a Kleist novella, trudging first this way, then that. They heard rumours of a hospital ship about to leave the port of Pillau on the Frische Haff lagoon, so they aimed for that. But when they arrived there, they were told that the ship was already overcrowded and about to cast off. Then somehow, two men with a stretcher appeared and, without explanation, loaded up Onkel Arnold. He insisted that he needed Franz to nurse him, and so even he was smuggled on board. Unlike a similar hospital ship which sank half-way across the Baltic because it was overloaded, they arrived safely in Rostock. That is only about 100 kilometres from Blunk. But, of course, Onkel Arnold knew nothing of the whereabouts of Tante Lena's trek. And so he headed south for their prearranged family rendezvous with relatives near Dresden. He dragged himself as far as Chemnitz before he collapsed and was admitted to a military hospital. When he contacted his relatives, he found out that at least two of his children – Kurt-Ulrich and Ilse – were there. Ilse, aged 15, had made her way from her school in Elbing on foot, transporting her suitcase on a stolen toboggan. They knew Tante Lena's new address. So as soon as Onkel Arnold recovered a bit, he dismissed himself from hospital in order to retrace his steps to the north. He and the children arranged to meet at Leipzig station. By coincidence they chose the very day on which Mutti and I, too, were passing through Leipzig; the day when Leipzig station was bombed out of action. So, of course, they failed to meet up. Onkel Arnold had no choice but to go on alone, without knowing what had happened to the children.

When Kurt-Ulrich and Ilse discovered that they couldn't go to Leipzig by train, they decided to hitchhike. They didn't even notice that the trucks they were trying to wave down were marked with the red Soviet star. They were put into a kind of prison-cum-refugee camp with Russian guards. Kurt-Ulrich, as ever, couldn't resist the sight of a gun and, when the guard left one leaning against the wall, Kurt-Ulrich picked it up. Not surprisingly, the guard didn't see the funny side of this. He shouted at Kurt-Ulrich and stood him against the wall, ready to shoot him. Or just to frighten him? As Kurt-Ulrich knew no Russian, and the guard no German, there was no way of finding out. But when another Russian soldier came into the room, an argument developed and, eventually, they let the boy go. Soon after that, the two children were sent packing (on foot!) to find their parents in the British Zone. Like Tante Lena before them, the Russians, too, found Kurt-Ulrich too much to handle.

Onkel Arnold didn't put up with the overcrowded conditions in their lodgings for long. He managed to get a little wooden hut allocated to their family, a kind of weekend home by the shore of a lake. And that's where they now live. They are still cramped, but at least they have a roof of their own, in a very picturesque setting.

Almost the next thing Onkel Arnold did was to sell one of his horses in exchange for a piece of land. Just a steep slope of rough pasture, not much good for anything; he lets a local farmer graze his cow on it free of charge. Whenever we go to Blunk, we're dragged up there to look at it. It's hardly bigger than the back lawn in Berschienen, but: "This is my land...," he says.

I expect Väti would have been the same.

XVII. FOR JUTTA - 1 JANUARY 1947

"We'll never laugh so much again in all our lives!" These are Mutti's exact words, spoken – of all times! – on New Year's Eve. How she can say such a thing beats me: half the time she walks around with tears brimming in her eyes. As for me, I feel quite worn out with unhappiness at times, and scheme to run away somewhere where nobody knows me or cares for me, and where I can just stop caring about anybody and anything. Big joke, that: where could you go to be happy?

But Mutti is right, in a way: we do find a lot to laugh about. Now that the seasons are coming round for the second time, we've stopped thinking of this place as a mere transit camp and are trying to become part of village life. It's become a standing joke among the locals here that all refugees claim to belong to the landed gentry of the east; and it's true that a lot of them do put on an irritating act of superiority to show that they've seen "better days". (Is it the same with you in the Russian Zone, or does everybody there try to impress their Communist masters with their "working class origins"?)

We don't want to belong to the show-offs, so we go to the other extreme and pretend to take everything in our stride. Easy enough for me: I've always preferred to go slumming with the labourers. But how Mutti thinks she can get away with it, I don't know. Did you know that before we left Mickelau she had never once peeled a potato? She tries so hard to keep her inexperience a deadly secret from the Brinkmanns, but with such limited success! And that's what makes it so funny. For example, when we work in the Brinkmanns' fields, she can't even drink her Ersatz coffee out of a bottle without dribbling!

The two of us sawing wood is like a scene from a comic film. We need fire wood because we cook on a funny little stove which is also supposed to heat the room; but as the smoke mostly refuses to go up the long black stove pipe and swirls round our heads instead, we have the choice between being warm and getting smoke-cured like salami, or opening the window and getting frozen to the marrow. We usually alternate between the two.

To get the wood, the Brinkmanns give us a lift on their horse cart to a forest nearby, where they are allowed to tidy up after the owners have felled trees for their own use. Good fun, that, a day in the woods, dragging branches about and lopping the side twigs off with a hatchet. The Brinkmanns aren't too particular about taking only the small branches that are meant for them. They smuggle a few fat ones into their pile, and we follow suit. Mutti looks so guilty that, if anyone were to challenge us, the blame would fall exclusively on her.

Anyway, we pay for our dishonesty later: the thick logs are, of course, much harder to saw into usable lengths. We perch them on the Brinkmanns' sawing horse and take up our positions at either side, each holding one end of the two-handed saw. The blade wobbles all over the place.

"Pull!" I shout – but invariably, we both pull at the same time. Or we do the wrong thing altogether: we push, and the saw buckles sideways in protest. When, by some miracle, we keep up the sawing rhythm long enough to make an impact on the wood, we find it impossible to control the direction of the blade and it goes

off in a spiral. As beginners, we then used to roll the whole log over and start from the other side, but we soon discovered that we merely duplicated our problem that way. A more promising alternative is to prop up the branch and bounce on it, trying to snap it. Most of the time, we lie in each other's arms, helpless with laughter.

Apart from wood, we also burn peat. Just as the Brinkmanns haven't got a copse of their own, they haven't a peat bog either. Instead, they go to a place nearby where, for money, you are given a piece of bog to work, and we tag along with them. That makes another nice outing. Luckily we don't have to cut the peat ourselves. That is done by the men with special long-handled knives. We merely stack the bricks, like children's building blocks, in pyramids to dry out. Frau Brinkmann entertains us with stories about how many children have disappeared here without trace, and how once the peat cutters came upon a human skeleton.

You can see how it could happen: the ditches are so deep and their sides so steep, you wouldn't stand a chance of climbing out. And the water is so black that you can never see the bottom. Needless to say, as a result, Mutti lives in perpetual fear that I might end up down there, whereas I am much more concerned about her fate.

It's surprising how self-sufficient you can become, even without owning any land. It makes you realize how wastefully we've lived up to now. When the Brinkmanns finish lifting potatoes, they harrow the field and pick up any potatoes that were left behind on the first go, just like we used to at home. But after that, they let us refugees have the run of the field, and you'd be astonished to see how many sacks we manage to fill. By going round the fields of several other farmers as well, we gather enough potatoes for winter eating, and some for making into potato flour. Grating the damn things is a hateful job, and I add plenty of skin off my knuckles to each bowlful of potato pulp. But it's fun to swish it around in water, to see the water turn cloudy and then clear, and then find the pure white starch settled at the bottom.

We also collect big basketsful of sugar beet. Frau Brinkmann allows us to use their pig food cauldron (scrubbed out, of course!) for boiling them down and making lovely black treacle. But you can't believe what a disgusting sickly stench we produce in the process.

Gleaning corn is no fun at all because it is so frustrating. You think you've got a lot when you've collected a sack-full of ears of wheat, but by the time the Brinkmanns have put it through the threshing machine for us, it's reduced to a small heap of grain. And when we take that to the mill in Heeslingen, a village nearby, where they weigh it most carefully and exchange it for the appropriate amount of flour, we're left with hardly anything at all. I'm convinced we're being cheated all along the line. But still, it's something for nothing – except, of course, time; and we have plenty of that.

Time, too, is all we need to gather a good supply of wild fruit. The hedgerows and woods are our only source of raspberries, blackberries and elderberries for making jam and juice – not like in Mickelau where we collected them for fun, just to have a change of flavour from garden fruit. Remember how we used to thread wild strawberries like beads on stems of grass?

92

During the bilberry season, the inhabitants of Freyersen organize an expedition to some distant forests. Tractor-Mayer gets out his tractor, and half the population of the village piles into the trailer. To our astonishment, everyone took several large milk churns with them, and offered us the loan of one, too. Believe it or not, Mutti and I just about filled it! Picking became so obsessive that I spent all night rushing from one good patch to another in my dreams.

Our real problem starts later: where to scrounge enough sugar for converting our harvest into jams and syrupy juices that we can live on for the rest of the year. The farmers have no such difficulties: you can swap anything on the Black Market for a chunk of ham or sausage. And not only in the local shops. Nowadays, there are streams of hoarders pouring through the village each weekend. They come hitch-hiking, or on the narrow-gauge train, which is working again, from Bremen, Hamburg and heaven knows where else. Sometimes, when we walk through the Brinkmanns' kitchen, I see them there, offering their wares: clothes, china, pots and pans, even antiques. It makes me think of the game we used to play: "Ich bin die Jüd'sche von Paris mit vielen schönen Sachen. Du darfst nicht sagen ja, nicht nein, nicht weinen und nicht lachen..."[17] But it's the sellers who seem to be close to tears sometimes. Herr Brinkmann usually looks quite embarrassed, but Frau Brinkmann drives a hard bargain, you can tell by her eyes. Afterwards, she'll ask Mutti's advice about whether she's been had. For all our chipped china and shoddy clothes, and for all Mutti's efforts to hide her "better days", Frau Brinkmann obviously has faith in Mutti's judgement of quality.

I hate these intruders from the towns. I know I should feel sorry for them: starvation in the towns is said to be terrible in our part of Germany, far worse now than during the last months of the war. Which isn't surprising when you consider that most of the farming land is in your Russian zone, and most of the people in ours. But as we refugees have no food to offer them, they have nothing to offer us; and they trespass on our hunting ground. The Brinkmanns have become meaner than ever with their payments in kind whenever I work for them. Just because we live in the same house, they increasingly take my help for granted. I don't mind much, because I like the work anyway. But if Mutti gets a chance, she prefers to work for people in neighbouring villages, even though that means a long walk on top of the hours at work. She weeds people's gardens, or she helps with the cooking, baking or jam making. Once, when a neighbour saw her set out, he said, "On your way then, odd-jobbing?" He used the word "scharwerken", the term which we had used in Mickelau to describe the lowest of low-paid jobs. It shocked me to hear it applied to Mutti, and I could see it upset her, too. But she pulled herself up and, looking every inch the Lady of the Manor, smiled, "Yes, if that's what you want to call it."

When Mutti wants to barter some possession of ours for food, she goes to great lengths to find customers other than the Brinkmanns. She recently lugged a

---

[17] "I'm the Jewish woman from Paris with many pretty things; you mustn't say yes and you mustn't say no, you mustn't cry and you mustn't laugh..."

horse's harness to a village seven kilometres away and came back with all sorts of goodies, including butter, sugar and eggs. She decided to celebrate her business prowess by baking a cake. She filled it with jam and squidgy "vanilla pudding" – a concoction of milk thickened with potato flour and flavoured with sugar beet treacle. It looked mouth-watering. Just as we sat down for our ceremonial feast, there was a knock at the door. Hospitality is a thing of the past. For one thing, it doesn't do to admit that you have something special ("What have they got to offer on the Black Market?" "Did they pinch the eggs from us?") For another, I for one was not prepared to share such a rare treat with any stranger... So Anneli whisked the cake into hiding. We have curtained off a corner of the room to make a kind of store; there we keep spare clothes and sheets and such like, in a pile of cardboard boxes. Anneli perched the cake on top of this tower before Mutti opened the door and welcomed our caller inside. As we sat there, making polite conversation, there was a sudden thud behind the curtain. The visitor spun round, startled. Anneli and I giggled. But Mutti carried on the conversation with great presence of mind: "Can't grumble... have happy children..." And she smiled benevolently at us. And afterwards, the cake – or as much of it as we could scrape off our winter woollies – tasted extra good.

I will say this for the Brinkmanns, though: they do have the odd fit of generosity. For example, when I had my confirmation, they bartered a basket of potatoes in exchange for a dress from one of the Hamburg hoarders. It's quite ghastly: black, with purple piping round the neck and cuffs. The material is a sort of horrible clinging crêpy stuff. But the custom here is to wear black, so I was grateful that I didn't have to go to church in a check gingham featherbed cover – our only source of dress material! Mutti says that black looks more like a funeral than a confirmation, and I think in that case I was the corpse: I look like death warmed up in black. On the other hand, old photographs of Anneli in her bridal white organdie confirmation dress look utterly ridiculous. Luckily I was spared the embarrassment of having my own photo taken, as all cameras were confiscated by the British at the end of the war.

The Brinkmanns don't have a threshing machine of their own. The farmers in the village take it in turns to rent one. They help each other to get as much of the work as possible done as quickly as possible. And so the Brinkmanns rope us in, too, in exchange for a bag of grain. Even Mutti came once. She looked so funny, swaddled in apron and scarves against the dust, and she wielded the pitchfork with such caution, as if she were afraid of it – which, of course, she was. But not half as afraid as I was of her using it.

She didn't last long. When someone stirred up a mouse's nest and the poor creatures scuttled across the floor of the barn, Mutti burst into tears and fled, as if pursued by demons. Everyone howled with laughter, I loudest of all. But really, I was ashamed of her... Poor Mutti. I suppose I should have followed her into the house to comfort her, but how could I leave my post on top of the threshing machine without bringing yet more disgrace on our family?

You'd think she would have got over her mouse hysteria by now. For weeks we've had a sweet little mouse live with us in our room. It became quite tame, in spite of Mutti's antics. She clambers shrieking from chair to table to bed, but it's

94

quite impossible for her to find a safe refuge. As each piece of furniture touches another, mice have a free run up and down and across in all directions. We didn't dare set a trap, for who was to empty it? Even I am squeamish about **dead** mice. Until, that is, the mouse started interfering with Anneli's dressmaking efforts. Anneli had cut up some old curtains and spent ages trying to stitch them together into a patchwork skirt. In between working on it, she stored it in the curtained-off corner of the room. Then, one day, when she pulled out her creation, it hung in shreds. We found bits of it made into a cosy little nest inside a cardboard box.

That night, we borrowed a trap. It clicked shut before we had even turned the light out. So that, I thought, was the end of our dear little mouse. But the gnawing sounds went on through the night as before. So we set the trap again. And again, and again, night after night. We stopped counting when we reached fifty. With our room being so choc-a-bloc with our possessions, you couldn't begin to look for the mouse hole. Anyway, the calm way in which Frau Brinkmann reacted to this episode made us realize that here, sharing your kitchen with mice is as acceptable as sharing your room with the cattle.

Remember how shocked I was when I first saw the Brinkmanns at their meal, with the frying pan on the table? That's become absolutely natural to us by now. As for eating the soup and meat course from the same plate, we've fallen into far worse habits to save washing up: we each keep our own plates and cutlery from one meal to the next, though stacking them into mouse-proof piles takes almost as long as the washing-up would. Almost! Washing up involves fetching water from the pump in the Brinkmanns' wash place, then stoking up the fire to heat it, clearing a space for the washing-up bowl and the dripping dishes, and then slish-sloshing all the way back to the pump to empty the bowl down the drain.

For some reason, Mutti still insists on using table napkins, I think mainly because she wants to justify having kept them through thick and thin on the flight from Mickelau. But instead of ironing them, we fold them neatly and put them under a cushion on a chair, and sit on them until smooth! The same treatment is given to everything except dresses. Very economical. I don't suppose Onkel Egon would allow such lowering of standards in your household. As for us, we only notice this when friends from our posh past visit us unexpectedly. Whether they ever give it a thought is another matter. After all, we're all in the same boat.

But we make a special effort whenever Anneli brings home one of the people she works with. We've got to keep up appearances with them, or they might think Germans don't know any better! Anneli has a proper job as interpreter with the British Military Government. She now lives in Zeven, in a beautiful furnished room all to herself at the local pharmacists'. I can't think why such a room hadn't been filled up with refugees ages ago, and I don't know how the British discovered it. It seems they can take over any building they fancy – in the same way as they had cleared out the Brinkmanns that time when we moved into the chicken hut.

At first, I found it a bit embarrassing that my sister lives in a requisitioned room. But the old couple seem to like her. Probably it's to their advantage, too, to have such contact with our present "occupation government".

It certainly is to ours: Captain Morrison, the commandant (by the way, he isn't English but Canadian, which isn't American as I had thought, but British! Can you make sense of that?) managed to scrounge some furniture for us from an old German army camp. So we replaced the Brinkmanns' monstrosity of a bed with a conventional-sized white iron one which looks less gloomy and also takes up less floor space. A side-effect of this improvement is that the tower of bedding now sits on a narrower base and is, therefore, even higher than before. You have to build it up in the mornings, rather like a hay load on a cart. At night, we dismantle some of it for my lair on the floor, and Mutti sleeps on top of the rest. One night she woke me up with a shriek, "Vorsicht!"[18] I sat up with a start, and a good job, too: a moment later my head would have been engulfed in an avalanche of eiderdowns, with Mutti amongst it. I don't know what the Brinkmanns thought of the hoots of laughter coming through the wall at three in the morning.

---

[18] Watch out!

XVIII. FOR JUTTA - APRIL 1947

We are the proud owners of a wireless. Well, "proud" is the wrong word; "apologetic" would be nearer the truth... The radio is another bit of booty from the ex-army camp which Anneli managed to scrounge for us. At first I thought it was wonderful. Washing up to music is nothing like as dreary as when you have to do it in silence. It's also a good way of learning English, because just about all the hit songs are in that language. Which isn't surprising: they could hardly go on playing, "Denn wir fahren gegen Engeland"[19]. Now we take "a sentimental journey... on a slow boat to China" and so on. I wonder if you, in the Soviet zone, have a revision course in the songs we learnt from the Russian prisoners in Mickelau?

Well, one day my enjoyment was spoilt by an unknown caller. He collared Mutti on her way through the Brinkmanns' kitchen and asked if he could talk to her. No, not at the Brinkmanns, but in private. So Mutti ushered him into our room, I cleared a chair for him, and he perched on it so awkwardly that I began to wonder whether I'd left too big a pile of laundry under the cushion. He talked a bit about the weather and his health, but he couldn't make himself spit out the real reason for his visit. His eyes swivelled round the room all the time as if he was searching for something. It was really creepy. And suddenly he got up and left, just like that.

We were completely mystified, until Frau Brinkmann explained: when the British soldiers had gone round the villages confiscating cameras and radio sets soon after the occupation, this man had lost his radio to them. So when he heard rumours about us being given furniture by the Military Government, he thought he might find his radio with us...

*This episode gave us quite a shock. Is this how our good fortune looks to other people: scrounging things from the Tommies which **they** have nicked from our fellow citizens! Luckily we know that our presents come from an army camp which doesn't really belong to anybody now; or does it? In any case, is it fair that we should have them, just because of Anneli's connections?*

And what does it mean, "fair"? We have such arguments about that, Mutti, Omi and me.

Yes, Mutti's mother now lives with us. We fetched her from Onkel Arnold's place in Blunk to slot her into the space that became empty when Anneli moved out. Much to everybody's surprise, she has survived the uprooting from East Prussia quite well; not just the hardships of the trek, but the homesickness since then. And yet she used to claim she was too old to travel the 30-odd kilometres from Alischken to Mickelau! The biggest problem is how to fill her time now that she hasn't got a farm to run. She's become quite good at peeling potatoes and always does ours, and sometimes a huge potful for the Brinkmanns (whereby she

---

[19] "For we're off to fight the Brits": the signature tune for special announcements of military triumphs during the war.

earns us a bowlful of potatoes in exchange: the first wages of her life?). She reads a bit, but most of the time she sits and thinks and talks about Alischken. Sometimes she makes us laugh at the contrast between there and here. At other times she gets me down – because, of course, everything was better in Alischken: the air smelt fresher, the weather was sunnier, the water tasted purer, and as for the people...

She thinks it is so unfair that she had to lose all that, and Mutti agrees with her. When I say we should blame Hitler for that, they say: but why should the refugees alone pay the price for the wrongs of the Hitler regime? Which is true in a way. But I get really annoyed when they carefully sort out various documents that prove what we used to own and what savings we used to have, etc. so that we can eventually be compensated for our losses. As if, just because we used to be better off than some of the refugees, we deserve to be better off now. Is that fair?

At the same time Omi talks about her regrets at the missed opportunities for all sorts of friendships with people at home with whom one simply wasn't expected to mix socially! The small farmers, the trades people, craftsmen... Such nice people, she says, and yet she never thought of inviting them for afternoon coffee and cake.

The good thing about Freyersen is that there's no such snobby division. All the farms are roughly the same size and, by East Prussian standards, very small (under 100 hectares). As everyone speaks Plattdeutsch, you can't draw distinctions by their speech, either. And even the farm hands and maids are usually just farmers' children working away from home for a year or so.

Marianne Brinkmann and her friends have been going to dancing lessons, and when it came to the grand ball at the end, they invited me. Big joke, I thought, visions of Anneli's first ball gown before my inner eye: wafting layers of pale turquoise tulle... How could I cobble together something comparable out of faded curtains from Mickelau! But then Marianne showed off her dress: a bright red cotton dirndl with a white blouse. And she looks lovely in it.

The ball itself didn't exactly take place in a grand ballroom with crystal chandeliers dripping off a tall ceiling, but in a dreary rectangle of a room attached to a pub: bare floorboards, and flimsy curtains flapping limply over poky windows. Our group from Freyersen walked the two kilometres there along the sandy track, so my clodhoppers weren't in the least out of place.

I didn't get many dances, though, and I kept thinking of Omi's story about a wallflower in her youth: the son of the house had nobly asked the plain girl to dance once, out of a sense of duty. Thereafter, whenever he walked vaguely in her direction, she would jump up and shout, "Here I am, here I am!" I felt like doing the same. To listen to Viennese waltzes and sit still is torment.

I stand a bit more of a chance of dancing at the Saturday night hops that take place on different farms in Freyersen. The barn-like aisle between cowshed and horse stable makes a good dance hall once you've removed the carts and pushed aside the chaff shredder and root shredder and other bits of farm equipment. You scatter chaff on the concrete floor to make it slippery, which is why these dances *are called "Hackesball[20]". Two of the farmers are good accordion players and take it in turn to provide the music.*

On those occasions, the most popular dances are "Bunte Tänze" – quite complicated folk dances that are traditional in this area. They are good fun, but I'm hopeless at them. I always know a bar too late when to twiddle where, and as for shrieking and clapping and shouting "Yuhuu!" at the top of my voice, I'd die of embarrassment...

It always reminds me of watching the Russian prisoners dance in Mickelau... The tunes were different, but my longing to take part was the same.

In my mind's eye, I see the dog-kennel-like prisoners' compound; I see the prisoners dancing to their heartbreakingly melancholy songs. We had been for a walk, a whole crowd of us – our family with a party of friends – and we had been attracted by the sound of music. We looked on from a polite distance, embarrassed to go closer, for how could we stand there, ogling, like at performing monkeys in a circus?

Vassili had no such inhibitions. Practical as ever, he demanded "Vodka!" with a disarming grin. Well, we didn't have vodka, but Mutti sent for a basket of eggs from the kitchen, and that, too, was found acceptable. Katya turned up at our side of the fence; her feet tapped, shoulders jerked, eyes flashed. Väti asked the guard to let her join the prisoners in the enclosure. And he, grim-faced with disapproval, locked the padlock again after her, as though they were all dangerous wild animals that might tear us apart. At that moment they almost seemed it, with their flying feet and flailing arms, their stamping and clapping and sudden exclamations.

Oh, how I longed to join in and be one of them...

The main reason why I don't have to sit out during the "chaff balls" is that I don't have to wait to be asked. I can take the initiative. It's quite normal on these occasions for two girls to dance together. A good job, too, for of course, there are many more girls than boys of dancing age about.

I only noticed that when it began to change. Until recently it had seemed quite normal that the only males you saw were either very old or decrepit, or kids in short trousers. (The "no fraternization!" British soldiers don't count.) But now some of the German soldiers who were taken prisoner in the last days of the war have been released. The Brinkmanns' oldest son, Heini, is one of those.

He is good fun, and fairly good-looking, too: a long narrow face with a long narrow nose and grey-blue eyes; wide mouth with lips that, for a man, are surprisingly definite in shape. Whenever we're working together on the farm, he laughs and jokes and teases me. The other day, after we'd finished milking and were alone in the dairy, he suddenly stopped in the middle of fooling about. He held me very still, and his face came closer and closer to mine. I saw him turn into a Cyclops – you know how we used to do it when we were children – and

---

[20] literally "chaff ball"

then, I don't know why, I shut my eyes. And felt his lips come straight onto mine, soft and sort of nuzzling, like a horse's nostrils. And his tongue, all moist and stiff, pushed between my lips straight into my mouth. I was horrified, but didn't know how to get it out again. I pushed with my own tongue, we went round and round each other and suddenly – oh horror! – I found my tongue in his mouth. It felt a bit like sticking your hand into a calf's mouth, only worse... nicer... confusing.

Luckily Marianne called him just then, and we shot apart. I was glad to get away. He reeked of milk – you know that ghastly cowshed smell at milking time... And yet, since then, I time my visits to the loo so as to go past him when he's having his wash under the pump.

The funny thing is that both Mutti and Frau Brinkmann try to put an end to our romance – I think for the same reason; or should I say, contrary reasons: that each isn't good enough for the other. Not that they say so outright. But Mutti keeps stressing the importance of a "good background" and "good education" in one's friends; and Frau Brinkmann makes a point of telling me about the dowries that the marriageable daughters collect in their bottom drawers.

As if thoughts of marriage entered my mind! If they did, it wouldn't be Mutti but Frau Brinkmann who would succeed in putting me off Heini, but not for the reason she thinks: I would hate to have a bottom drawer. I hate possessions! This is something I felt more strongly each time I had to wrench myself away from a few more of my precious belongings during our trek. I've discovered that there are very few things you really need, and that everything else is useless clobber. And that gives me a lovely sense of freedom. I hope I'll never lose that.

XIX. FOR JUTTA - AUTUMN 1947

My school report calls my behaviour "satisfactory", and my participation in lessons "lively". Well, that's one way of looking at it.

It took ages before schools started up again in our zone, much longer than in your Soviet zone. Unlike the Russians, the British don't seem to have thought of training German refugees from the Hitler time to become teachers after the war. This meant that all the old teachers had to go through a process of "denazification" before they could become re-employed. I think of them like a disinfected dairy herd in quarantine after an outbreak of foot-and-mouth disease. They've come up with some strange specimens at the end of it, I can tell you!

There was an added reason for the delay in opening the only secondary school within my reach: for ages, the British army used the building for their barracks. Even now we have to share the classrooms in shifts with the primary school. Ours is a so-called Mittelschule, with a Mittlere Reife as a school leaving exam. But as far as I can work out, for most of the pupils it's not so much middle as end stage of education. The main idea seems to be to turn us into clerks and secretaries. We learn shorthand, and we were supposed to learn typing, but there aren't any typewriters.

At first I really hated it. Even if I don't know what I want to be, I do know that I have no intention of ever taking an office job, thank you very much. Also, after nearly two years of freedom (the soup kitchen sessions in Bautzen hardly count as school, do they!) I don't fancy such a step back into childhood: sit down, stand up, put your hand up, don't shout out, don't look at your neighbour's work, don't cheat... But then I thought, OK, if you want me to be childish, I will be childish! Now I've discovered that behaving irresponsibly is enormously enjoyable.

My best friend is a girl called Ilka. She comes from Hamburg. When her family were bombed out, she and her mother moved to Zeven. She has beautiful brown eyes and blond hair, is very self-confident (or conceited, depending on how you look at it) and always ready to have fun.

*Our first coup was to grab two seats in the far back corner of the classroom. "You can't sit there," all the others said, "that's the **boys'** side." "Who says?" we said and sat tight. Nobody had an answer to that, so we were allowed to stay.*

Eventually we made friends with the two boys in the seats in front of us, which is rather surprising. They get into no end of trouble because of us. The other day we surreptitiously tied one of them to his chair, and when he stood up to answer a question, the chair stuck to him, which Ilka and I found hilarious, even if nobody else did.

Another time we organized a general exodus during a sewing lesson. The boys go out to play football during that period, which we think is unfair: why do only girls have to stay indoors with boring needlework? Our teacher is a refugee woman from the Baltic. She made the mistake of bragging to us about her past work at the household of a Latvian countess: "And sometimes she let me have her discarded clothes..." When we pressed her to describe this aristocratic garment, it was nothing more than a vest! We didn't forgive her for disappointing our romantic expectations.

Well, during this particular lesson we all, one after another, asked "to be excused" until she sat there on her own. She never even seemed to notice. So eventually we crept back into the room and agreed that she was even dopier than we'd thought. But Mutti thinks it shows the opposite, and that she tackled our silly prank very skilfully.

Zeven

Another friend of mine is Waltraud, a refugee girl who lives in the village next to Freyersen. She and I are the only people from this parish who go to the Zeven school: the locals don't hold with education beyond the compulsory village school level. We usually travel to Zeven by the little rail bus. As this often runs late, we use this as an excuse even on the rare occasions when it's on time. So we nearly always skive the first lesson. Instead, we play infantile games of hopscotch behind the church, or we build dams in a nearby stream. Or we go into town to do the family shopping, to save time after school. We don't even bother to hide our bulging shopping bags when we arrive at the school, panting our apologies for the train being late yet again. In fact, I would positively enjoy being found out. My main aim in school is to annoy my teachers.

I can't help feeling this is not what Väti had in mind when he was so keen on my education. But I doubt whether he would have approved of the Zeven school set-up. Lessons are so boring! Mental arithmetic, dictation, spelling, lists of

102

English vocabulary, learning boring passages by heart: "Kent is the garden of England..." Who cares? Give me milking or mucking out any day!

One of the problems is that we have hardly any text books. To "denazify" them is even more time consuming and complicated than cleaning up the teachers. And this applies not just to German readers and history books. According to Waltraud, some maths books used to set problems about how many useful citizens you could support for the price of maintaining one mental patient in hospital and similar topics. Is she exaggerating, or was I too thick to notice?

I don't remember any Nazi indoctrination from my school years in Insterburg. Of course, there was the morning ritual of singing the national anthem with arms raised in the Hitler salute, but that was more likely to encourage sedition than support. All those tricks we invented for propping up our flagging arms!

In History lessons, my class never progressed beyond Ancient Rome and the Byzantine Empire. I don't know whether that was deliberate or due to the fact that my schooling came to an end before we reached "Modern Germany" in the syllabus? Our teacher used to tell us passionate stories of poison plots and intrigues and faithful friendships between masters and slaves, husbands and wives, and she allowed us to act out playlets in front of the class. Once, we actually moved her to tears with our performance, but even then we didn't make fun of her. Was it true that she was nicknamed "Red Clara" because she was a Communist? If so, why was she allowed to go on teaching us history, of all subjects?

I made myself listen to radio reports on the War Crimes Trials in Nuremberg. All those unimaginable atrocities... Do you realize that so many of our "war heroes" picture collection turn out to be involved, one way or another? I am so horrified, I can hardly bear to think about it.

Do I carry some of the blame for it, just because I am German? Our British rulers seem to think so. I hear them talk again and again of our "collective guilt". I find that hard to accept: hard to think of myself as one with the local inhabitants here, and in Schwarzenberg, and in Bautzen; hard **not** to think of myself as belonging to the people of Mickelau, whatever nationality – German, Russian, Belgian, Polish, the lot! And harder still to feel responsible for atrocities I didn't even know were happening.

But... was the reason for not knowing that I didn't **want** to know?

I have a horrible half-memory of an afternoon long ago in Mickelau. Anneli had rung up to say that she was coming home from Insterburg in the middle of her school week. Something unusual must have happened. Mutti and I drove to the station in the barouche to meet her. On the way back, Anneli kept on talking and sobbing, and I didn't have a clue what it was all about – something concerning a synagogue that had been burnt. I didn't know what a synagogue was, but the grown-ups were so upset, it seemed best not to ask, best not to bother. So I crawled under the rug and went to sleep. Was that the infamous "Kristallnacht" of November 1938, when Jewish shops and houses and synagogues were smashed up all over Germany?

Now, just at the time when I'm trying to sort out my ideas, along comes my hateful form teacher, Herr Zwink, and tells us to be "proud of being German". How he slipped through the denazifying net, I don't know.

I suppose I have never consciously thought about being German. As far as I know, none of us did, at home. Was that because we in East Prussia never quite belonged to Germany, what with being separated from the "Reich" by the Polish Corridor[21] for most of our history? Or was it because we country yokels never gave a thought to issues beyond next year's harvest? Was Mickelau our "fatherland"?

I asked Herr Zwink what he meant by Germany: is East Prussia included? (From what we hear, that province is now split crossways: the northern part, including Mickelau, belongs to the Soviet Union, the lands south of Mickelau to Poland.) What about all the other areas that used to belong to the "Great German Reich" – the Polish Corridor, Austria?

*Zwink looked at me with his cold cruel eyes and shut me up with biting sarcasm: "Ex oriente lux!" (Before you reach for your Latin dictionary, let me tell you that you won't find the proper translation there. What **he** means is, "Shut up, you nasty little worm from the east!" He doesn't believe in discussions. He told us he had "never had any discipline problems until you refugees arrived on the scene".*

I think he has a special dig at me even in singing lessons, where we sing song after song about the Lüneburg Heath. Once I asked him if we could sing "Ännchen von Tharau", which is about where I come from, and he said that was hardly relevant now… So Ilka and I sing it with gusto, just to annoy him. I've also taught her the East Prussian anthem, "Land der dunklen Wälder und kristallnen Seen…"[22] which we hope is to Zwink like a red rag to a bull.

Do you know what he said to me the other day? "You're so fat, you're getting fatter every day, and your poor mother is fading away… Have you no consideration for her, that you deprive her of her fair share of the food?" He achieved his purpose: there, in front of the whole class, my tears came streaming down my face. I just couldn't hold them back. He's absolutely right, that's the worst of it. But you know how stubborn Mutti can be: short of force-feeding her like a goose before Christmas, I don't know how to make her eat more.

Zwink knows about Anneli from her days as interpreter for the British Military Government in Zeven, and he has it in for me because of her, too, suggesting – in class! – that she is, at best, a turncoat, and at worst, a you-know-what. To be honest, I don't know precisely what. I suspect it has to do with my naivety again.

What would he think if I told him about Tristan?

---

[21] the strip of land that gave landlocked Poland access to the Baltic Sea
[22] "Land of dark forests and crystal-clear lakes"

The man who changed our lives

Tristan in his armoured car

That story began just before the official end of the war. Anneli and Rita had gone to Zeven. They were walking because there were no trains running in those days. On the way back, a British army lorry stopped and offered them a lift. They sat among a group of soldiers in the back. One of them (called Tristan, of all the funny names!) was particularly interested when Anneli mentioned that she wanted to be a journalist, because that was his job, too. He was also intrigued by the story of Vitya. Good material for an article? He took Anneli's address, and a few evenings later, he came pedalling along on a bike to meet Vitya. He took some photographs and then went off.

Well, after that, we forgot about Tristan. But in October, an armoured car drove into the village and stopped near Marianne Brinkmann. A soldier popped his head out at the top, produced a photograph of Anneli and Vitya and asked Marianne whether she knew these people. Marianne says she had visions of Anneli being transported off to jail in a sort of tank! She hummed and hah'ed, but was too scared to say no, and in the end directed him to us.

And so Tristan turned up again. Far from coming to arrest Anneli, he offered her a job with his army newspaper, the "News Guardian", in Lübeck. At first, Anneli was a bit suspicious of his motives. I think she remembered that other soldier with his promise of chocolate. But when he agreed to employ her friend, too, she accepted the offer. So she is now living in Lübeck.

As a side effect of these developments, she is arranging for me to go to the Grammar school there next year when I reach the end of the middle school at Zeven.

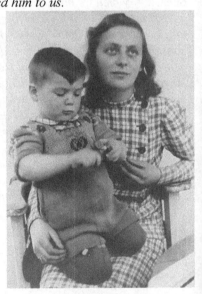

Vitya and Anneli

XX. FOR JUTTA - 22 OCTOBER 1948

It's no use, I can't talk to you any more; I no longer know what to say to you. Isn't it ironic that this should happen now, at the very time when we can actually post letters to each other instead of waiting for a possible reunion!

*The reason isn't just that we haven't seen each other for so long, although heaven knows, three and a half years **is** a long time. To think that I was a mere kid of 14 when we were last together in Schwarzenberg – what a nerve I had to consider myself adult then! So, of course, we both must have "matured", as Mutti would call it (like smelly Tilsiter cheese?).*

It isn't that you're too far away, although it feels like it, and I have to use a map to convince myself that there are hardly more than 100 kilometres between Freyersen and your new home in Gardelegen, about the same distance as between Freyersen and Lübeck, which has become a frequent weekend trip for me.

I think it is mostly because that new frontier between us blocks even my thoughts of you. By drawing this arbitrary line, bang through the middle of Germany, from the Baltic to Czechoslovakia, our conquerors have managed to divide you and me between two hostile camps!

"Hostile" is no exaggeration, as far as the British are concerned. I can hardly believe my ears sometimes: weren't the Russians their allies in the war? Now, the British haven't a good word to say for them.

Jutta   **Anneli and Marlene**

Do you know that, in a way, the war isn't over yet: the Allies can't agree on who should sign a peace treaty for Germany. It seems the British, Americans and French have their own ideas about the new Germany, and the Russians have different ones, and they can't reach a compromise. The way things are going, the West will soon go ahead with plans for a separate West German state, regardless of Stalin's reaction.

There are even rumours that these one-time allies want to fight against each other. It shocks me how much support there is for this notion in our neighbourhood. Perhaps you can excuse the Brinkmanns and their likes: in this village backwater they've never known how horrible war is: to them it just means the inconvenience of having refugees dumped in their houses. The only way they see of ever getting rid of us is to send us back to where we came from. And as the Russians don't allow that, it can only be done by force.

But that some of the refugees, too, should be in favour of another war – with half our relatives and friends on the other side – that I find unbelievable. How could any amount of homesickness justify more death and destruction?

I wish I knew how you feel about it. Do you consider the Russians your new oppressors, as they are presented to us? Or are the Western Powers the new warmongers in your eyes? Do you think of us Germans in the British Zone as your new enemies? The way people talk here, all inhabitants of the Russian zone are Stalinists...

When I left Freyersen last April to go to school in Lübeck, Omi told me not to take more luggage than I could carry, in case I had to take to my heels yet again, Lübeck being only just outside the Russian Zone!

Of course, I had never been to any frontier, let alone this new one, and I was curious to see what such a thing looked like. So one day I made an excursion to the Baltic coast and scrabbled about among the sand dunes east of Travemünde. How could I tell a British Zone sand dune from its Soviet counterpart? I think I half expected to see a line drawn in the sand with a stick, the way we used to mark the boundary between two teams in games of "Völkerball" at home in the farmyard. Certainly I wasn't prepared for anything so dramatic as the muzzle of a gun pointing at me as I rounded another hillock. I clearly saw the Soviet star on the soldier's cap. He shouted something at me. An Alsatian dog barked. There were coils of shiny new barbed wire stretched out among the spiky marram grass.

*For a moment, I stood paralysed with fear. Then I became furious. I, who thought I hadn't a trace of patriotism in me, was outraged because here, right across German soil, someone had set up a frontier. "How dare you!" I wanted to shout back at the guard, "This is **one** country, all of it!" Needless to say, I didn't. I turned in my tracks and ran as fast as I could go. Away from this barrier between you and me.*

They call it the "Iron Curtain".

~~~~~

The Iron Curtain made contact between Jutta and me difficult for a long time, and it took years before I knew the full story of her experiences during that period. The more bizarre details of the events she was living through remained unknown even to her until much later.

After Mutti and I had left Schwarzenberg that spring morning in 1945, the Kowalewskis debated whether they too should pack up yet again and travel north. Most of their relatives and friends from East Prussia seemed to have been sluiced there. But rumours of chaos caused by bombing raids and the general collapse of the Reich discouraged any decision. So they drifted along, waiting for the enemy to arrive – whether from the east or the west, they weren't sure. By all accounts (although they knew that none were reliable) the American and Soviet armies were equidistant from the town, and the sound of artillery fire came from both east and west. The Kowalewskis kept their fingers crossed that the Americans would get there first. After all, they had spent the last seven months with the aim of escaping the communist hordes!

The wholly unexpected thing happened: no one came. The German capitulation was proclaimed over the radio on 8 May. Then – silence. No sound of fighting, no air raids, no traffic on the roads, let alone enemy tanks. Even the constant hum of the factories stopped. Perfect peace. It could have been enjoyable had it not been for the hunger. There was no food, not even the meagre rations that they had learnt to live with. Schwarzenberg, this industrial and mining area, didn't produce any food. And outside supplies could not reach them. So it went on day after day. Had the world totally forgotten them?

What had happened was this: in order to avoid shooting at each other by mistake, the Soviet and the American military commands had agreed that they would halt their advance at the boundary of the Schwarzenberg district; but they forgot to specify whether this referred to the eastern or western border! And so it came about that for three weeks after the end of the war, an area about 30 kilometres in diameter remained unconquered. Unknown to the rest of the world, a small group of opponents of the Hitler regime – communists, Social Democrats and Jews who, for a variety of reasons, had survived the Nazi time – got together and formed a sort of mini state which they called "the Republic of Schwarzenberg". Despite the general confusion and chaos, they administered it according to almost Utopian principles of democracy and justice. It couldn't last. Once the Allies discovered their blunder, the diplomatic tug-of-war between the Soviets and Americans began. The Soviet Union won and belatedly occupied the district, and the Republic of Schwarzenberg was wiped almost completely from historic records.

Before long, the Russians discovered a most coveted mineral in local mines: the uranium for the first Soviet atom bomb came from the mountains of Schwarzenberg.

No wonder I had found the landscape sinister.

XXI. LÜBECK - 1948-1949

My admission to the Secondary school in Lübeck had not been straightforward. There was an entrance examination, and the school authorities were appalled by my results. It required special pleading by Mutti, reinforced by the headmaster (although **not** by my form teacher!) of the school in Zeven: the two-year gap in my formal education, together with the general upheaval in my life... Eventually the headmaster of the Ernestinen Girls School was prepared to give me a provisional chance.

I loved the school. It was the most stimulating environment I had ever been in. The building itself made me feel very scholarly with its wrought iron entrance, its arched corridors and grand, church-like assembly hall, complete with organ.

Ernestinen School, Lübeck

The other girls in my form struck me as admirably sophisticated and well-informed. They could talk politics and morals, painting, music and poetry with the same ease as I would discuss milk yields and fertilizers with Herr Brinkmann. As a consequence of this, lessons were much more stimulating than in Zeven.

The teaching of German literature included visits to the recently reopened theatre. Afterwards, we were encouraged to criticize both play and performance. We read Lessing, Kleist and Keller and argued about social justice, tolerance and world peace.

I, who had always prided myself on my ability to write, now discovered that this was of little use if I had nothing worth saying. While I strung words together in my essays, some of my class mates wrote literature – or so it seemed to me.

Instead of the interminable Hermann Löns songs about the Lüneburg Heath which had filled our music lessons in Zeven, we sang Schubert and Mozart and Schütz, we were taught about fugues and counterpoint, about sonatas and symphonies, and were taken to evening concerts and even an opera.

I regretted the wasted years in my musical education. In my parents' eyes, I had shown promise as a child prodigy: at an early age I had played the German national anthem, including the Nazi addition of the "Horst Wessel Song", by ear, picking out the tune on our piano with due reverence, with one finger! I did not live up to this early promise during the two years of formal piano lessons in Insterburg, when I constantly had my knuckles rapped by the frustrated teacher.

At mid-morning, we were herded into the school basement with bowl and spoon to queue for our "Hoover school meal" – a portion of Sauerkraut or raw carrots, a ladleful of chocolate custard or rice pudding with raisins: a gift from the American nation to the undernourished school children of West Germany for which we were not always grateful.

By the time I moved to Lübeck, Anneli had gone to Berlin to work with the German correspondent of the English Sunday paper, "The Observer". I took over her room in the home of a cheese merchant. I loved the sense of space with a room of my own and I didn't feel lonely in the least, even though I was expected to eat all my meals on my own. There was always enough to eat, especially cheese! One weekend, when I was hitchhiking back to Freyersen with my parcel of sandwiches, the smell of cheese became overpowering. I was about to apologize to the driver who was giving me a lift in his lorry, when he said, "Sorry about the pong, my lorry is full of cheese."

On my short visits to Freyersen, without the irritation of being permanently cooped up there, our little room felt very much like home: the familiar wool-embroidered "Kelim" table cloth from the Mickelau sitting room, the old dining room curtains shortened to half their length, and the warm presence of Mutti... Part of me always wanted to stay, but the other part longed to get away. I felt increasingly sorry for Mutti. Without any of her children about, the place closed in on her and Omi like prison walls. But she never showed the least sign of bitterness, just excitement on our behalf – Anneli's and mine.

In June, Anneli went on a visit to England, as guest of the family with whom she was working in Berlin. While she was out of the country, an astonishing change took place in the western part of Germany: the Currency Reform. Overnight, the old money from the Hitler days became replaced by the brand new Deutschmark. It was as if a fairy had waved her magic wand over the drab shop windows and transformed them into gleaming displays of luxury goods. No one seemed to know where they came from. The prices seemed ridiculously low until you remembered that each new Mark was worth more than fifteen Reichsmark. I could hardly wait to show Anneli this miraculous development on her return from England.

I met her at the air terminal in Hamburg and took her to an elegant cafe where proper coffee made from coffee beans was now served, instead of the Ersatz coffee of roast rye, and real cream cakes instead of custard-filled ones. To my disappointment, Anneli hardly noticed.

"Guess what I've brought you," she said, and didn't wait for my answer, "An invitation to go to University in England!"

"Haha," I replied, "Look, it's genuine cream!"

But she waved a piece of paper under my nose. It was very official looking, with an exotic crest and a heading consisting, at first glance, of nothing but consonants and y's – the letter that in German word games is always the hardest to get rid of. COLEG PRYFYSGOL CYMRU ABERYSTWYTH, it said, and underneath, "Fräulein Marlene Wiemer has been invited to attend the University of Wales, Aberystwyth, and therefore urgently requires the necessary travel documents."

Anneli explained that it was Tristan's father who had arranged this. He was the man described in the letter heading as the "*llywydd*"[23]. He had talked some of his

---

[23] the president

110

rich friends into paying for my university education in Britain. I would be living with him.

To Britain

Claus visited by Tristan while a POW in Scotland, and with Marlene at Street Acre, Tristan and Anneli's Kentish home

"Rubbish!" I said angrily. Having so recently been brought face to face with my own ignorance, among girls who were themselves two years away from any qualification for university entrance, I knew it was a pipe dream. Besides, I was happy in Lübeck and wasn't at all sure that I wanted to leave. But Anneli insisted that one could not turn down a chance like this, and anyway, it was too late to back out. She worked on my self-confidence for so long that, by the time I had the necessary visas and identity documents, I knew I was God's gift to the University of Wales.

And so, on 8 January 1949, Mutti and Anneli saw me off at the Hamburg air terminal. I felt no pain at parting from them, no last-minute regrets. My heart pounded, but only because alternate waves of joy and fear about what the future might hold washed over me. The plane hopped and bumped over the runway like an old crow getting ready for flight. Then, all at once, I was suspended in the air. Below me, houses and trees became small and insignificant, like toys that I had outgrown. And so, it seemed to me, did all my past life. I was off and away, of my own free will, to new and exciting adventures. And the first of these was being sick into an airways paper bag.

XXII. POSTSCRIPT – NEW SKATERS AT THE EDGE OF THE WOOD

August 1993

My expectations of "new and exciting adventures" were borne out by most of my subsequent life. But my early past never became "small and insignificant".

The so-called "Cold War" between Eastern Europe and the West, which followed the end of the fighting of the Second World War, meant that Mickelau was out of bounds for me for almost 50 years. Even contact between the two halves of Germany was difficult. Once, when I tried to visit Jutta in 1972, I was turned back at the border because my papers were not in order. (I had by then a British passport). A second attempt in 1978 with my British husband and three children was more successful, although the border crossing was still made difficult. The desolate stretch of no-man's land, sanitized and bare of any vegetation, coils of razor wire punctuated by tall watchtowers, guard dogs patrolling among the forests, passport controls – one after another, after another, after another, all executed by robot-like officials… Together, they were enough to put off any casual tourist. When our small son wanted to pee, we dared not stop in open country to let him go behind a tree. We asked an official at the next control post for the way to the toilets. He replied brusquely, "There is no provision for this sort of thing here…"

Mutti's 80th birthday with her three children

In 1980 we applied for permission for Jutta to come and visit my mother in West Germany on her 80th birthday. Our request was refused that time, and again in 1986, when we knew that my mother was dying. The reason given for the refusal was that she was not a "blood relation". Officialdom could not cope with the fact that the ties that bound Jutta to my mother were stronger than any blood, especially since the death of Jutta's own parents.

Mutti's ashes floating in the Baltic Sea 1990

My mother would have loved to be buried in East Prussia. As she knew this was impossible, she asked for the nearest possible alternative – that we should tip her ashes into the Baltic Sea near Lübeck, in the hope that some particle of her might wash ashore among the sand dunes of the *Kurische Nehrung*[24].

Yet only two years later everything changed almost overnight. After Gorbachev introduced "Glasnost", the Iron Curtain began to lift. Tourists from Eastern Europe were allowed to visit the West, and tourists from the West were not only allowed to travel to Eastern Bloc countries; they were actually encouraged. For example, one could now go to the southern part of East Prussia that had become part of Poland.

But still not to Mickelau. Even after the unification of the two German states, and after the dissolution of the Soviet Union, that particular corner of the new Russia, the Kaliningrad enclave, remained closed to outside visitors. The ostensible reason was the lack of hotels suitable for tourists; the fact that the area had been one of the main military territories of the Soviet Union probably also had something to do with it. By a strange coincidence, this land which, when German, had been cut off from its national seat of government (in Berlin) by the so-called Polish Corridor, had again lost its geographical connection with its national seat of government (in Moscow) after the collapse of the Soviet State – in this case, because Lithuania gained its independence from Russia.

At last, in 1993, Jutta and I made plans to go back as tourists. After our close relationship in the past, it was only right that we should face the return together.

---

[24] the narrow strip of land that separates the lagoon from the Baltic Sea

We decided to travel by road – coach, bus and taxi. This meant that we travelled through four different regions that in our childhood were called Germany but for almost fifty years since then had belonged to separate states: the former West Germany, the former East Germany, Poland, and the former Soviet Union, now Russia.

Red Army burial site memorials

"The memory of the fallen soldiers killed in the Ozyorsk region
during the Great Patriotic War 1941-45 will be sacred for us forever"

From the superficial impressions gained by looking out of a bus window and by brief overnight stops, I could see no signs of a past identity common to all. Only in the Polish land east of the Vistula did I recognize the East Prussia of my past, caught in a time warp: little homesteads with beautifully tended cottage gardens of flowers and vegetables, single cows tethered in a corner of an unfenced meadow, farmers with scythes and old-fashioned horse-drawn agricultural machinery and carts – just like the peasant farms near Mickelau fifty years ago; except that many of the cottages displayed TV aerials and even satellite dishes!

During our journey, there had been a gradual progression from the affluence of West Germany to ever greater frugality. But the difference between the Polish and Russian parts of East Prussia was stark. As soon as we had crossed the border from Poland, the friendly gardens and little fields were replaced by a vast expanse of sparse grassland, on which big herds of cattle and sheep were watched over by cowherds on horseback. There were few buildings, and most of these, whether modern or left over from the German period, were dilapidated.

What really thrived in this landscape were the storks. This had always been stork country. We had encouraged the stork families to settle on the farm by fastening an old cart wheel to the top of the cow shed roof, to serve as a platform for their nest. It had obviously been an unnecessary gesture. Now, with not so many roofs and, as far as I could see, no cartwheels to choose from, the storks nested everywhere: on dead trees, on derelict chimneys, on water towers, and on whole rows of telegraph poles.

During nearly fifty years, my memory of Mickelau had been allowed to set, without the intrusion of new impressions to obscure the past. It was like one of those pieces of amber from the Baltic in which an insect had been trapped and preserved perfectly for all time. But my perceptions had been those of a thirteen year old. Would I be able to recognize the reality at all?

Whatever happened, I said, I would recognize the birch avenue leading from the main road to the farm. But when my brother Claus visited our home the summer before me, he came back with the news that the avenue was no more, and that the old buildings, too, had all but disappeared. I was forewarned.

All that is left of the birch avenue in Mickelau

1993 – one solitary tree   2014 – nothing but a track

In 1993, the nearest hotels to Mickelau were on the Baltic coast – the very area where my mother had hoped her ashes would wash up. We stayed in one of these hotels and took a taxi all the way to Mickelau. It was a journey of about three hours.

I wasn't (consciously) sad or anxious. I was able to have a perfectly coherent conversation with the German speaking Russian taxi driver, with Jutta and with Peter, my husband. But for some reason, tears were streaming down my face like rain falling from the sky. I could have sworn I wasn't crying.

That was until we came to the farm drive. There were, after all, still a few birch trees left, but they were broken and stunted. The surface of the drive was overgrown and pitted with puddles. My father had been obsessed with drainage, and whenever I had walked around the farm with him, he had taught me to drain puddles from tracks by dragging my heel through the mud towards the ditch. My father and I hadn't walked here for a long time.

There was a strand of barbed wire spanned across the drive, blocking our way; naturally, since there was no other fencing, and there was a cow herd visible in the distance. But to me, this barbed wire was like a personal rejection: I was unwelcome and unwanted at my old home. I howled aloud.

Dimitri, the taxi driver was discreetly sympathetic. He had been here before, several times: to this very place, with Claus, with Anneli, with my cousins Usch and Annelore. And he had been witness to many similar, emotionally charged,

115

homecomings in other places since the beginning of the post-Gorbachev "nostalgia tourism". It was his new income and good fortune.

We walked up the drive to where I still somehow expected the farm to come into view behind the lilac bushes. Where the house should have been, there was a bank of nettles and brambles. Leading up to it were five ugly concrete steps. They must be the most photographed ugly steps in the world: Claus has them in his album, so has Anneli, so now have Jutta and I – the only variation being who is photographed sitting on them! These used to be the steps leading up to the wooden veranda and front door. That they should be the only part to survive!

The farmhouse steps, then and now

As they once were – Claus on Illyrier

Jutta, Peter and Marlene in 1993

With children and grand-children, 2014

I remember the arguments between my parents when the old wooden steps became rotten and unsafe. My mother wanted them to be replaced by new wooden ones that were in keeping with the veranda; my father insisted on brick and concrete which would last forever. Little did he know...

The horse stables and cow shed could still be identified by a few half walls of stone. But the final demolition was obviously in progress, as there were stacks of

116

old bricks and stones waiting for collection. Of the other farmyard buildings, I could see hardly any sign, and when we came upon odd bits of foundation, I couldn't place them. I was confused by scale in this emptiness, and by the unaccustomed unimpeded views right to the skyline of peat bog and forest. It was a revelation to see how soon history can become archaeology.

The pond behind the cowshed, where I had taken the horses to drink and in which I learnt to swim, had become a slimy stagnant puddle. The bigger pond in the meadow where we had liked best to skate had disappeared altogether into a marshy grassland area. I began to wonder whether my father's annual work on renewing and repairing the drainage system of the land had been more essential than I understood at the time. Perhaps this was the root cause of the general change of the landscape from arable to wetland and steppe.

On our explorations, we came across two young men with a sausage dog that could have been an illegitimate relation of my beloved Maya. No, they told me in response to my question, they were not the owners; and no, they didn't live here: they had just come mushrooming. That, at last, made me feel at home. I described to them in my halting Russian how, in the days when we lived here, we used to set out early in the morning while the dew was on the fields; how we used to go there and there and there... Where were the best places now, I wanted to know. But like mushroomers all over the world, they were cagey about giving away that information.

One of the men told us that his aunt had lived in Mickelau in the days when it was a collective farm. She now lived in a neighbouring village which still had a working collective. He gave us direction on how to find her.

It was perhaps not surprising that Antonya Mukhina turned out to be such a sympathetic and understanding person: she, too, had had the experience of being uprooted from her home – repeatedly, and under much more traumatic circumstances.

During the German occupation of her home town in Central Russia in the 1940s, she had been taken from her family to work in a factory somewhere in Germany. She didn't know where, nor what was being made in the factory. Child that she then was, she must have been completely bewildered in this hostile environment, where she did not even know the alphabet of the language used around her. As she lived in a camp, she didn't pick up any German apart from a few commands and swearwords.

When she returned home at the end of the war, she found that everything had been destroyed by the retreating German troops. Then she and many others in the same predicament were sent to settle in the newly annexed province of Kaliningrad. That is how she came to live on our farm about a year after we had fled from it. By then, the farm had been turned into a collective, and twenty-odd families were settled there. But most of the buildings, fields and gardens seem to have been almost as we had abandoned them. The children plundered the same apple trees as I had. They played on the same veranda, and eventually went to the same village school (with different teachers!) in the neighbouring village. Gradually, my home became their home, and they grew new roots. "Your house was so beautiful," said Antonya.

117

And then came Gorbachev's perestroika. The collective farm became a private cattle range, which meant that the old work force was no longer needed. So the families had to move yet again. The old farm buildings and cottages became useful only as building material.

Antonya and her clan of relatives (she was by then a grandmother) were sent first to a dilapidated old German cottage, and then to the newly built quarters of a collective farm in a village three miles away. That is where they made us welcome. Antonya and her daughter Galya with three children lived in one of the houses. Two of her sons and families lived almost next door.

Antonya and family

Galya and her eldest daughter, Ira, took us on a tour of the village. Of course, I had known it in my childhood, but I could hardly remember it. In any case, it had changed beyond recognition. There was the modern collective farm complex which gave employment to nearly all the inhabitants. The only motorized traffic that I saw was tractors and the farm milk tankers. There was a kindergarten. There was also a new school which, I was told, took the place of the one in the neighbouring village that I (and, more recently, Galya) had gone to.

And there was even a very smart big supermarket. I expressed admiration. "Come and look," said our guides, holding their sides with laughter. Through the big shop front, we saw racks and racks of shelves... with nothing on them except, in one corner, about a dozen tins, all of the same kind! I couldn't make out what it was, but it must have been something really useless, for the doors of the shop were firmly locked. "This is perestroika," Galya told us, laughing. She added, as a sort of apology for being amused by what was clearly a disaster, "Never mind, we manage somehow. We're always a happy family!"

The remaining old German buildings were also pointed out to us, and we were introduced to some of the current occupants. The houses were mostly in a state of collapse. As the labourers of the collective had their own modern quarters, I assume that the old houses belonged to people without a proper income who therefore had no money to renovate them. Their gardens were a wilderness of soft fruit. We were invited into several of them to help ourselves to raspberries, gooseberries and redcurrants.

Just as our farm labourers in Mickelau used to have a few cows and pigs of their own, so did the labourers on the collective. Somewhere at the far end of the village, we joined other householders as each fetched their cow from the Collective herder, who took care of them during the day. It reminded me of collecting the children from primary school in our English village.

One of the unfamiliar looking buildings on the collective farm that was pointed out to us was the communal bath house. Had we ever had a proper Russian bath, Galya wanted to know, for we would certainly have one today: her brother Victor was already preparing it!

Before long, Victor appeared, with a very threatening looking bundle of birch branches in his hand. He led away my bemused husband Peter amid general laughter. Our friends and their extended families didn't use the farm bath house, but their very own log cabin. Peter re-emerged after about an hour, battered but glowing and exhilarated. He had discovered one bit of language with which he could communicate: "Sehr gut!" He was also proud to have found out that if you are taken short during a sauna, you simply pee through the floorboards. As far as I could see, this didn't apply to the women's session when our turn came!

The best memory of the visit, however, came from the next morning's walk with Natasha, Galya's twelve-year-old daughter. She led us to the village where I had gone to school, and where the ruin of the school house still stood near its orchard. The track that had been my daily route to school was totally gone, and there was no time to explore ways through the wilderness that would have led us to Mickelau by the back way: our taxi would soon be waiting for us.

So we just walked back the way we had come. Natasha picked wild flowers and fruits for us. She told us their names and medicinal properties; she talked about her school, her friends and the people we met, and about the recent changes that were bringing uncertainty to their lives.

"I think she is like I imagine you fifty years ago," said Peter when we were travelling home, with a bunch of shrivelled wild flowers on my knees and a jar of wild fruit conserve between my feet. "Here's the whole country on the brink of disaster – and Natasha collects herbs as if nothing else matters. She belongs here."

CHRONOLOGY

8 March 1931	Marlene born
30 January 1933	Hitler becomes Chancellor of Germany
12 March 1938	Austria is declared to be part of German Reich
September 1938	Munich conference between Britain, France, Italy and Germany. Hitler is allowed to annex Sudetenland, the German-speaking part of Czechoslovakia.
9 November 1938	"Kristallnacht" – synagogues and Jewish shops are destroyed
15 March 1939	German troops occupy Prague and the rest of Czechoslovakia
22 March 1939	Hitler annexes Memelland from Lithuania
31 March 1939	Great Britain guarantees to support Poland in event of German aggression
23 August 1939	German-Soviet pact of non-aggression; agreement to divide Poland between them
1 September 1939	Hitler invades Poland from north and west. Then Stalin invades Poland from east.
3 September 1939	Britain, France, Australia and New Zealand declare war on Germany
March 1940	Finland surrenders to USSR after winter of war. The other Baltic States surrender to USSR without fight.
April/May 1940	Germany invades Denmark, Norway, Holland, Belgium and Luxembourg
10 May 1940	Germany invades France
May/June 1940	British troops evacuate from Dunkirk
22 June 1941	Germany attacks USSR: Operation Barbarossa
December 1941	USA joins war after attack on Pearl Harbour
2 February 1943	German army at Stalingrad surrenders
6 June 1944	D-Day: Western Allied troops land in Normandy
20 July 1944	Plot to assassinate Hitler fails
27/28 July 1944	Soviet planes bomb Insterburg; Marlene's school holidays extended indefinitely
18 October 1944	Call-up of People's Militia (Volkssturm)
22 October 1944	Mickelau trek leaves home
29 October 1944	Mickelau trek settled in the village of Ebersbach
8 November 1944	Väti sentenced to serve in People's Militia
10 January 1945	Mutti escorts Marlene to Bautzen
20 January 1945	Mutti leaves Bautzen to return to Ebersbach
23 January 1945	Mickelau trek evacuated from Ebersbach
11 February 1945	Yalta Communiqué about planned post-war division of East Prussia
13 February 1945	British air raid destroys Dresden
17 February 1945	Kowalewskis and Marlene evacuated from Bautzen to Schwarzenberg, in the Erzgebirge
21 March 1945	Poste Restante address near Hamburg set up for the Mickelau trek

4 April 1945	Mutti arrives in Schwarzenberg to fetch Marlene
10 April 1945	Mutti and Marlene arrive in Freyersen
25 April 1945	Soviet and US forces meet at Torgau on the Elbe
8 May 1945	Unconditional surrender of German High Command; VE day
2 August 1945	Potsdam Conference. Yalta plans for division of East Prussia put in place: north to be part of Soviet Union, south to be part of Poland. Mickelau becomes Suchkovo as part of the Soviet Union.
6 August 1945	USA explodes atom bomb at Hiroshima.
7 October 1945	German Democratic Republic (GDR) created
1947/48	All remaining Germans expelled from Kaliningradskaya Oblast, the Soviet part of former East Prussia
1945-1989	"Iron Curtain" separates Eastern Europe from Western Europe; it prevents Marlene and Jutta from meeting.
8 January 1949	Marlene goes to university at Aberystwyth
October 1989	Berlin Wall breached by people power
August 1993	Marlene, Peter and Jutta visit Mickelau/Suchkovo

MAIN CHARACTERS IN THE STORY

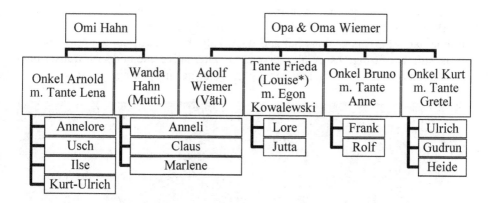

*Tante Frieda is called Louise in the text to avoid confusion with Frieda the maid.

Some of those living and working on the farm, as they were known to Marlene:

Fräulein Genzer	Cook/housekeeper
Frieda	Chambermaid
Hilde	Kitchen maid
Herr Bormann	Farm inspector
Horst & Günter	Farm apprentices
Gerda	Farm secretary
Heiland & family	Farm foreman
Otto Eichert & family	Coachman
Schalonka & family	
inc. Auguste Schalonka	Frau Schalonka's sister, Frieda's mother
Old Schwarz	Pig man
Young Schwarz & family	
Richard Siemanovski & family	Dairyman; later Frieda's husband
inc. Ursel Siemanovski	(Marlene's friend)
Haupt & family	Tractor driver; Hilde's parents
Kowalies & family	Shepherd
inc. Irene Kowalies	(Marlene's friend)
Brodin	Wheelwright
Hela and Katya	Ukrainian women brought as forced labour
Nikolai, Gregór, Vassili, Karp, Ivan	Some of the Red Army prisoners of war who were Marlene's particular friends
Biernacki family (daughter = Halina)	Forcibly resettled Poles
Lebrun, Fernand, Raymond	Belgian prisoners of war
Mosin family: Opa, Volodya, Vitya	Russians fleeing the Red Army

PLACE NAMES

Thousands of farms, villages and towns were renamed by the Nazi authorities in 1938 and the Soviet authorities in 1946. These changes can be researched online (e.g. at gov.genealogy.net and www.kalte-heimat.de) but as shown below, it is still confusing, especially given the alternative methods of transcribing Cyrillic into Roman letters, and general irregularities in spelling.

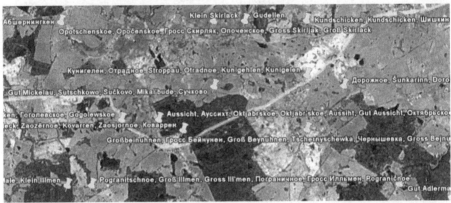

Here are the most common versions of the main places occurring in this book:

Old Prussian	New German	New Russian	Romanized/Polish
Alischken	Walddorf	Карпово	Karpovo
Angerapp	Klein-Angerapp	Рапа	Rapa
Aussicht	–	Октябрьское	Oktyabr'skoe
Berschienen	Birklacken	Прудки	Prudki
Beynuhnen	Beinuhnen	Чернышевка	Chernyshevka
Danzig	–	–	Gdansk
Darkehmen	Angerapp	Озёрск	Ozyorsk (Ozersk)
Ebersbach	–	–	Stare Siedlisko
Elbing	–	⌐	Elblag
Gelbsch	–	–	Giełpsz
Gumbinnen	–	Гусев	Gusev
Insterburg	–	Черняхóвск	Chernyakhovsk
Königsberg	–	Калининград	Kaliningrad
Kowarren	Friedeck	Заозёрное	Zaozyornoe
Lenkehlischken	Gutbergen	Гоголевское	Gogolyevskoe
Mikalbude	Mickelau	Сучково	Suchkovo
Osznagorren	Adlermark	Отпор	Otpor
Prassen	–	–	Prosna
Rossitten	–	Рыбáчий	Rybachy
Skirlack	–	Опоченское	Opochenskoe
Trempen	–	Новостроево	Novostroyevo
Wormditt	–	–	Orneta

MAPS

Numerous online maps (see links at http://j.mp/SkatingYeo or http://ozaru.net) demonstrate the ever-changing boundaries of East Prussia, and the turmoil it underwent during successive wars. Many are in Cyrillic script, and best viewed in high resolution and colour, but they should still be understandable as shown here.

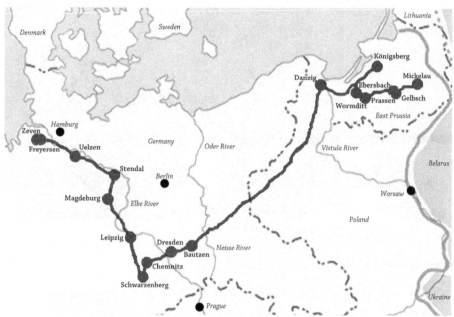

Marlene's trek, 1944-45 (detailed version available online)

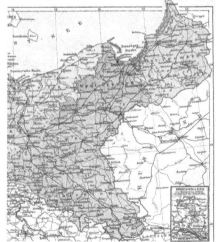

West and East Prussia in around 1905

Germany during the Weimar Republic / Third Reich, showing the Polish Corridor

124

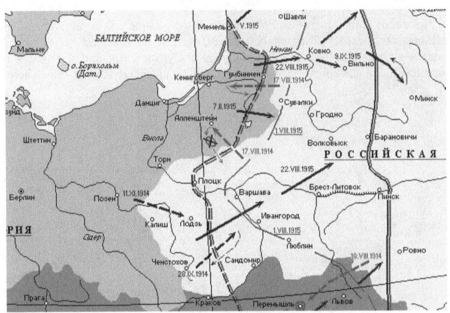

Area around East (and West) Prussia in 1914

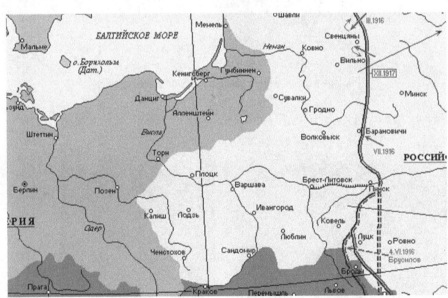

Same area showing extended Eastern Front in 1918

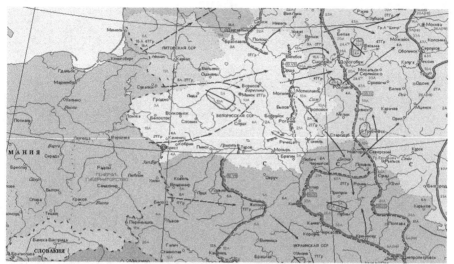

Eastern Front in 1941; Bratislava is bottom left, Moscow top right.

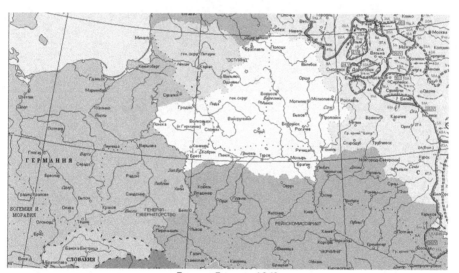

Eastern Front in 1942

English version: Eastern Front in 1941-42

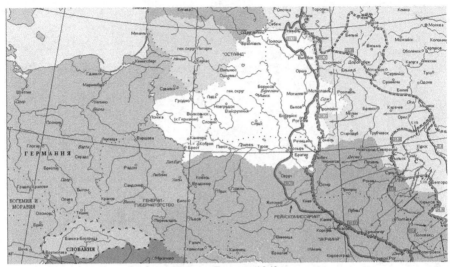

Eastern Front in 1943

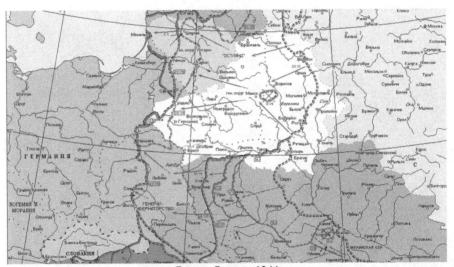

Eastern Front in 1944

English version: Eastern Front in 1944

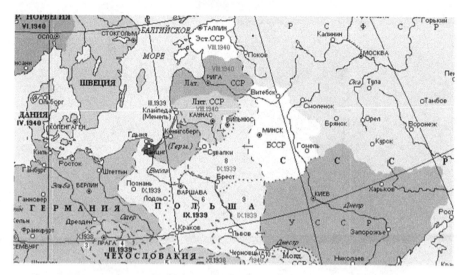

Poland, Danzig, East Prussia, the Baltic States, Belarus and Ukraine in 1941-42

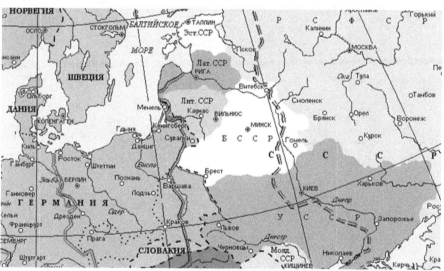

The same area as above, in 1943-44

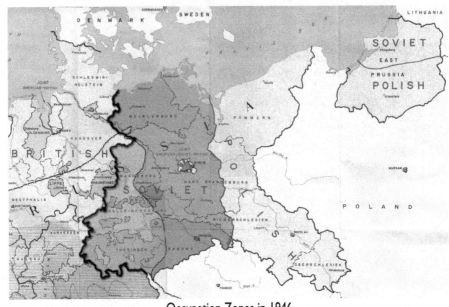

Occupation Zones in 1946

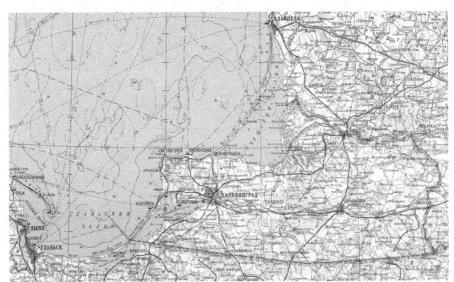

Soviet map of Kaliningradskaya Oblast, 1990

LIST OF PHOTOGRAPHS

FURTHER READING

(Various online links are provided at http://j.mp/SkatingYeo or http://ozaru.net)

Works in English (including translations from German):

Reflections in an Oval Mirror
Anneli Jones (née Wiemer: Marlene's sister)
See "Other Publications from Ōzaru Books" below

Before the Storm: Memories of My Youth in Old Prussia
Marion Countess Dönhoff, translated by Jean Steinberg
Alfred Knopf 1990 (ISBN 978-0394582559)

The Past is Myself
Christabel Bielenberg
Corgi 1988 (ISBN 978-0552990653)

When I Was a German: An Englishwoman in Nazi Germany 1934-1945
Christabel Bielenberg
University of Nebraska Press 1998 (ISBN 978-0803261518)

East Prussian Diary – a journal of faith, 1945-1947
Count Hans von Lehndorff
Wolff 1963 (Amazon ASIN B0000CLPTH)

From East Prussia to North Yorkshire
Hans-Dieter Hundsdoerfer
Old Hall Publishing 2006 (ISBN 978-0955271205)

Ursula – my other life
Pat Skinner
Malvern 1986 (ISBN 978-0947993139)

Flight of the East Prussian Horses
Daphne Machin Goodall
David & Charles PLC 1973 (ISBN 978-0715360613)

Forgotten Land: Journeys Among the Ghosts of East Prussia
Max Egremont
Picador 2011 (ISBN 978-0330456593)

Works in German:

Adlig Gut Alischken
ed. Wulf Dietrich Wagner
Supplement to "Ostpreussisches Bauen", August 1994, Karlsruhe

Namen Die Keiner Mehr Nennt
Marion Gräfin Dönhoff
Diederichs Eugen 2004 (ISBN 978-3896314413)

Weit ist der Weg nach Westen
Tatjana Gräfin Dönhoff
Nicolai'sche Verlagsbuchhandlung 2004 (ISBN 978-3894792152)

Menschen, Pferde, weites Land
Hans Graf von Lehndorff
Beck C. H. 2001 (ISBN 978-3406481222)

Kindheitserinnerungen aus Ostpreußen
Bettina von Arnim
Husum Druck 1987 (ISBN 978-3880423527)

In langer Reihe über das Haff
Patricia Clough
Deutsche Verlags-Anstalt 2004 (ISBN 978-3421051295)

Als die Deutschen weg waren
Adrian von Arburg, Wlodzimierz Borodziej, Jurij Kostjaschow
Rowohlt Taschenbuch 2007 (ISBN 978-3499622045)

Ein Land so weit
Petra Reski
List Taschenbuch 2002 (ISBN 978-3548601540)

Die grosse Flucht: Das Schicksal der Vertriebenen
Guido Knopp
Econ 2002 (ISBN 978-3430155052)

Im Galopp nach Ostpreußen
Heidi Sämann film about rebirth of the Weedern Trakehner stud

OTHER PUBLICATIONS FROM ŌZARU BOOKS

Reflections in an Oval Mirror
Memories of East Prussia, 1923-45
Anneli Jones

8 May 1945 – VE Day – was Anneliese Wiemer's twenty-second birthday. Although she did not know it then, it marked the end of her flight to the West, and the start of a new life in England.

These illustrated memoirs, based on a diary kept during the Third Reich and letters rediscovered many decades later, depict the momentous changes occurring in Europe against a backcloth of everyday farm life in East Prussia (now Russia's north-west corner, sandwiched between Lithuania and Poland).

The political developments of the 1930s (including the Hitler Youth, 'Kristallnacht', political education, labour service, war service, and interrogation) are all the more poignant for being told from the viewpoint of a romantic young girl. In lighter moments she also describes student life in Vienna and Prague, and her friendship with Belgian and Soviet prisoners of war. Finally, however, the approach of the Red Army forces her to abandon her home and flee across the frozen countryside, encountering en route a cross-section of society ranging from a 'lady of the manor', worried about her family silver, to some concentration camp inmates

"couldn't put it down... delightful... very detailed descriptions of the farm and the arrival of war... interesting history and personal account" ('Rosie', amazon.com)

ISBN: 978-0-9559219-0-2

Carpe Diem
Moving on from East Prussia
Anneli Jones

This sequel to "Reflections in an Oval Mirror" details Anneli's post-war life. The scene changes from life in northern 'West Germany' as a refugee, reporter and military interpreter, to parties with the Russian Authorities in Berlin, boating in the Lake District with the original 'Swallows and Amazons', weekends with the Astors at Cliveden, then the beginnings of a new family in the small Kentish village of St Nicholas-at-Wade. Finally, after the fall of the Iron Curtain, Anneli is able to revisit her first home once more.

ISBN: 978-0-9931587-3-5

Travels in Taiwan
Exploring Ilha Formosa
Gary Heath

For many Westerners, Taiwan is either a source of cheap electronics or an ongoing political problem. It is seldom highlighted as a tourist destination, and even those that do visit rarely venture far beyond the well-trod paths of the major cities and resorts.

Yet true to its 16th century Portuguese name, the 'beautiful island' has some of the highest mountains in East Asia, many unique species of flora and fauna, and several distinct indigenous peoples (fourteen at the last count).

On six separate and arduous trips, Gary Heath deliberately headed for the areas neglected by other travel journalists, armed with several notebooks... and a copy of War and Peace for the days when typhoons confined him to his tent. The fascinating land he discovered is revealed here.

"offers a great deal of insight into Taiwanese society, history, culture, as well as its island's scenic geography... disturbing and revealing... a true, peripatetic, descriptive Odyssey undertaken by an adventurous and inquisitive Westerner on a very Oriental and remote island" (Charles Phillips, goodreads.com)

ISBN: 978-0-9559219-8-8

West of Arabia
A Journey Home
Gary Heath

Faced with the need to travel from Saudi Arabia to the UK, Gary Heath made the unusual decision to take the overland route. His three principles were to stay on the ground, avoid back-tracking, and do minimal sightseeing.

The ever-changing situation in the Middle East meant that the rules had to be bent on occasion, yet as he travelled across Eritrea, Sudan, Egypt, Libya, Tunisia and Morocco, he succeeded in beating his own path around the tourist traps, gaining unique insights into Arabic culture as he went.

Written just a few months before the Arab Spring of 2011, this book reveals many of the underlying tensions that were to explode onto the world stage just shortly afterwards, and has been updated to reflect the recent changes.

"just the right blend of historical background [and] personal experiences… this book is a must read" ('Denise', goodreads.com)

ISBN: 978-0-9559219-6-4

Ichigensan
– The Newcomer –
David Zoppetti

Translated from the Japanese by Takuma Sminkey

Ichigensan is a novel which can be enjoyed on many levels – as a delicate, sensual love story, as a depiction of the refined society in Japan's cultural capital Kyoto, and as an exploration of the themes of alienation and prejudice common to many environments, regardless of the boundaries of time and place.

Unusually, it shows Japan from the eyes of both an outsider and an 'internal' outcast, and even more unusually, it originally achieved this through sensuous prose carefully crafted by a non-native speaker of Japanese. The fact that this best-selling novella then won the Subaru Prize, one of Japan's top literary awards, and was also nominated for the Akutagawa Prize is a testament to its unique narrative power.

The story is by no means chained to Japan, however, and this new translation by Takuma Sminkey will allow readers world-wide to enjoy the multitude of sensations engendered by life and love in an alien culture.

"*A beautiful love story*" (Japan Times)

"*Sophisticated... subtle... sensuous... delicate... memorable... vivid depictions*" (Asahi Evening News)

"*Striking... fascinating...*" (Japan PEN Club)

"*Refined and sensual*" (Kyoto Shimbun)

"*quiet, yet very compelling... subtle mixture of humour and sensuality...the insights that the novel gives about Japanese society are both intriguing and exotic*" (Nicholas Greenman, amazon.com)

ISBN: 978-0-9559219-4-0

Sunflowers
– Le Soleil –
Shimako Murai

A play in one act
Translated from the Japanese by Ben Jones

Hiroshima is synonymous with the first hostile use of an atomic bomb. Many people think of this occurrence as one terrible event in the past, which is studied from history books.

Shimako Murai and other 'Women of Hiroshima' believe otherwise: for them, the bomb had after-effects which affected countless people for decades, effects that were all the more menacing for their unpredictability – and often, invisibility.

This is a tale of two such people: on the surface successful modern women, yet each bearing underneath hidden scars as horrific as the keloids that disfigured Hibakusha on the days following the bomb.

"a great story and a glimpse into the lives of the people who lived during the time of the war and how the bomb affected their lives, even after all these years" (Wendy Pierce, goodreads.com)

ISBN: 978-0-9559219-3-3

The Body as a Vessel
Hijikata Tatsumi's Ankoku Butō
MIKAMI Kayo

An analysis of the modern dance form
Translated from the Japanese by Rosa van Hensbergen

When Hijikata Tatsumi's "Butō" appeared in 1959, it revolutionized not only Japanese dance but also the concept of performance art worldwide. It has however proved notoriously difficult to define or tie down. Mikami was a disciple of Hijikata for three years, and in this book, partly based on her graduate and doctoral theses, she combines insights from these years with earlier notes from other dancers to decode the ideas and processes behind butō.

ISBN: 978-0-9931587-4-2

Turner's Margate Through Contemporary Eyes
The Viney Letters
Stephen Channing

Margate in the early 19th Century was an exciting town, where smugglers and 'preventive men' fought to outwit each other, while artists such as JMW Turner came to paint the glorious sunsets over the sea. One of the young men growing up in this environment decided to set out for Australia to make his fortune in the Bendigo gold rush.

Half a century later, having become a pillar of the community, he began writing a series of letters and articles for Keble's Gazette, a publication based in his home town. In these, he described Margate with great familiarity (and tremendous powers of recall), while at the same time introducing his English readers to the "latitudinarian democracy" of a new, "young Britain".

Viney's interests covered a huge range of topics, from Thanet folk customs such as Hoodening, through diatribes on the perils of assigning intelligence to dogs, to geological theories including suggestions for the removal of sandbanks off the English coast "in obedience to the sovereign will and intelligence of man".

His writing is clearly that of a well-educated man, albeit with certain Victorian prejudices about the colonies that may make those with modern sensibilities wince a little. Yet above all, it is interesting because of the light it throws on life in a British seaside town some 180 years ago.

This book also contains numerous contemporary illustrations.

"profusely illustrated... draws together a series of interesting articles and letters... recommended" (Margate Civic Society)

ISBN: 978-0-9559219-2-6

The Margate Tales
Stephen Channing

Chaucer's Canterbury Tales is without doubt one of the best ways of getting a feel for what the people of England in the Middle Ages were like. In the modern world, one might instead try to learn how different people behave and think from television or the internet.

However, to get a feel for what it was like to be in Margate as it gradually changed from a small fishing village into one of Britain's most popular holiday resorts, one needs to investigate contemporary sources such as newspaper reports and journals.

Stephen Channing has saved us this work, by trawling through thousands of such documents to select the most illuminating and entertaining accounts of Thanet in the 18th and early to mid 19th centuries. With content ranging from furious battles in the letters pages, to hilarious pastiches, witty poems and astonishing factual reports, illustrated with over 70 drawings from the time, The Margate Tales brings the society of the time to life, and as with Chaucer, demonstrates how in many areas, surprisingly little has changed.

"substantial and fascinating volume... meticulously researched... an absorbing read" (Margate Civic Society)

ISBN: 978-0-9559219-5-7

A Victorian Cyclist
Rambling through Kent in 1886
Stephen & Shirley Channing

Bicycles are so much a part of everyday life nowadays, it can be surprising to realize that for the late Victorians these "velocipedes" were a novelty disparaged as being unhealthy and unsafe – and that indeed tricycles were for a time seen as the format more likely to succeed.

Some people however adopted the newfangled devices with alacrity, embarking on adventurous tours throughout the countryside. One of them documented his 'rambles' around East Kent in such detail that it is still possible to follow his routes on modern cycles, and compare the fauna and flora (and pubs!) with those he vividly described.

In addition to providing today's cyclists with new historical routes to explore, and both naturalists and social historians with plenty of material for research, this fascinating book contains a special chapter on Lady Cyclists in the era before female emancipation, and an unintentionally humorous section instructing young gentlemen how to make their cycle and then ride it.

A Victorian Cyclist features over 200 illustrations, and is complemented by a fully updated website.

"Lovely... wonderfully written... terrific" (Everything Bicycles)

"Rare and insightful" (Kent on Sunday)

"Interesting... informative... detailed historical insights" (BikeBiz)

"Unique and fascinating book... quality is very good... of considerable interest" (Veteran-Cycle Club)

"Superb... illuminating... well detailed... The easy flowing prose, which has a cadence like cycling itself, carries the reader along as if freewheeling with a hind wind" (Forty Plus Cycling Club)

"a fascinating book with both vivid descriptions and a number of hitherto-unseen photos of the area" ('Pedalling Pensioner', amazon.co.uk)

ISBN: 978-0-9559219-7-1

The Call of Cairnmor
Sally Aviss

Book One of the Cairnmor Trilogy

The Scottish Isle of Cairnmor is a place of great beauty and undisturbed wilderness, a haven for wildlife, a land of white sandy beaches and inland fertile plains, a land where awe-inspiring mountains connect precipitously with the sea.

To this remote island comes a stranger, Alexander Stewart, on a quest to solve the mysterious disappearance of two people and their unborn child; a missing family who are now heirs to a vast fortune. He enlists the help of local schoolteacher, Katherine MacDonald, and together they seek the answers to this enigma: a deeply personal journey that takes them from Cairnmor to the historic splendour of London and the industrial heartland of Glasgow.

Covering the years 1936-1937 and infused with period colour and detail, The Call of Cairnmor is about unexpected discovery and profound attachment which, from its gentle opening, gradually gathers momentum and complexity until all the strands come together to give life-changing revelations.

"really enjoyed reading this – loved the plot... Read it in just two sittings as I couldn't stop reading." (P. Green – amazon.co.uk)

"exciting plot, not a book you want to put down, although I tried not to rush it so as to fully enjoy escaping to the world skilfully created by the author. A most enjoyable read." (Liz Green – amazon.co.uk)

"an excellent read. I cannot wait for the next part of the trilogy from this talented author. You will not want to put it down" (B. Burchell – amazon.co.uk)

ISBN: 978-0-9559219-9-5

Changing Times, Changing Tides
Sally Aviss

Book Two of the Cairnmor Trilogy

In the dense jungle of Malaya in 1942, Doctor Rachel Curtis stumbles across a mysterious, unidentifiable stranger, badly injured and close to death.

Four years earlier in 1938 in London, Katherine Stewart and her husband Alex come into conflict with their differing needs while Alex's father, Alastair, knows he must keep his deeper feelings hidden from the woman he loves; a woman to whom he must never reveal the full extent of that love.

Covering a broad canvas and meticulously researched, Changing Times, Changing Tides follows the interwoven journey of well-loved characters from The Call of Cairnmor, as well as introducing new personalities, in a unique combination of novel and history that tells a story of love, loss, friendship and heroism; absorbing the reader in the characters' lives as they are shaped and changed by the ebb and flow of events before, during and after the Second World War.

"I enjoyed the twists and turns of this book ... particularly liked the gutsy Dr Rachel who is a reminder to the reader that these are dark days for the world. Love triumphs but not in the way we thought it would and our heroine, Katherine, learns that the path to true love is certainly not a smooth one." (MDW – amazon.co.uk)

"Even better than the first book! A moving and touching story well told." (P. Green – amazon.co.uk)

"One of the best reads this year ... can't wait for the next one." (Mr C. Brownett – amazon.co.uk)

"One of my favourite books - and I have shelves of them in the house! Sally Aviss is a masterful storyteller [... She] has obviously done a tremendous amount of research, judging by all the fascinating and in-depth historical detail woven into the storyline." ('Inverneill' – amazon.co.uk)

ISBN: 978-0-9931587-0-4

Where Gloom and Brightness Meet
Sally Aviss

Book Three of the Cairnmor Trilogy

When Anna Stewart begins a relationship with journalist Marcus Kendrick, the ramifications are felt from New York all the way across the Atlantic to the remote and beautiful Scottish island of Cairnmor, where her family live. Yet even as she and Marcus draw closer, Anna cannot forget her estranged husband whom she has not seen for many years.

When tragedy strikes, for some, Cairnmor becomes a refuge, a place of solace to ease the troubled spirit and an escape from painful reality; for others, it becomes a place of enterprise and adventure – a place in which to dream of an unfettered future.

This third book in the *Cairnmor Trilogy*, takes the action forward into the late nineteen-sixties as well as recalling familiar characters' lives from the intervening years. *Where Gloom and Brightness Meet* is a story of heartbreak and redemptive love; of long-dead passion remembered and retained in isolation; of unfaltering loyalty and steadfast devotion. It is a story that juxtaposes the old and the new; a story that reflects the conflicting attitudes, problems and joys of a liberating era.

"the last book in Sally Aviss's trilogy and it did not disappoint ... what a wonderful journey this has been ... cleverly written with an enormous amount of research" (B. Burchell – amazon.co.uk)

"I loved this third book in the series ... the characters were believable and events unfolded in a beguiling way ... not too happy ending for everyone but a satisfying conclusion to the saga" (P. Green – amazon.co.uk)

ISBN: 978-0-9931587-1-1

Printed in August 2023
by Rotomail Italia S.p.A., Vignate (MI) - Italy